To
Geord

Love Janice
xx
x

Love
UNBOXED

An Anthology
BY WOMEN
FOR WOMEN

Compiled and Published by

Placida Acheru

WITH A COLLECTION OF
HEART-SEARCHING TRANSFORMATIONAL WOMEN

http://bookprojects.uk

Disclaimer
This book is to educate and provide general information.
The author and compiler has taken reasonable precautions
in the preparation of this book and believes that the facts
presented were accurate at the time of writing.
The author and compiler specifically disclaims any
liability resulting from the use or application of the
information contained in the book.

PRAISE FOR LOVE UNBOXED

Much more than a romantic novel. In ´Love Unboxed´ you´ll read incredible love stories that marked the lives of different women. Enter a vortex of passion and desire that will captivate you from the first line. Each personal story could be your own, your unique fantasy or perhaps, a restrained woman yet to be discovered. Live a unique literary experience from the hands of these women writers who will guide you to your own identity: the adventure of being a woman.

-Victoria Calvo: Author of Independence Ties. A novel about an indomitable woman who fought in the War of Independence.

Not every day one finds a book full of life. Books are written to induce people to imagine, find fantasy worlds full of characters and recreated stories, worlds that take them to unthinkable places. *Love Unboxed* will invite you to take a journey to the most remote places of your being, it will drive you through truth to the best place one can find: the empowerment of love.

Every story told in this marvellous book tells the initiation journey, the life story of women who fight, who live, who work, who feel, who transform love into the greatest tool of massive construction that exists.

Without a shadow of a doubt, a unique experience that will not leave you unmoved.

-Jose' Luis Fuentes: CEO AlientaCoaching, Master Coach, Writer, International Speaker.

In this book are true examples of a wholehearted life's, where the passion for self-love and the wish to benefit others is evident. Their shared experiences are beautifully inspirational, illustrating how one can be found in toxic relationships only to find that one has a choice: to let go of all the preconceived concepts we are fed and the conditional ways of relating, and to realise that everything we need is right here within us—in, of, as and through Love.

-Madalena Alberto: Singer and West End actress (Evita, Cats) madalenaalberto.com

'Love Unboxed' is a beautiful collection of heart-felt stories from women who show courage, vulnerability and insights and in doing so learn to grow into making better choices and speaking their truth. This book illustrates women perfect in their imperfections having the capacity to transform challenging experiences to serve as guidance in the future, not shackles of their past.

This book will encourage women everywhere and give them the strength to acknowledge the inner voice they must trust in their own discernment & their great capacity for total restoration, no matter how wounded they have been.

It's a fantastic read!

-Natalie Ledwell: Best Selling Author and Co-Founder of Mind Movies LLC.

DEDICATION

This book is dedicated to the women who have inspired me through their acts of bravery.

To Aunt Peggy, who transformed her life from zero to hero. From you I learned the importance of financial independence and leaving a legacy for your children. If you can see it, you can achieve it.

To Lady Comfort Ohia, a woman who overcame the turbulence of marriage by sticking to her marital vows for the sake of her children and the man she loved. I am in awe of your strength, courage and wisdom.

To my latest inspiration, ***Colette Tate*** aged eighty-three, who looked after her first husband through twenty years of heart-breaking illness, for him to die at aged sixty-one, then after having not being on a plane since her honeymoon, flying to Tasmania over ten thousand miles away, learning to ski at seventy-two and remarrying at seventy-five, to now be touring the world with her new man.

This dedication would not be complete without mentioning ***Monica Acheru***, my mother. At seventeen married, and after four children almost lost my father, to another woman. She kept her faith in God, praying for twelve years that he would return, and return he did. They are now still together today for a total of fifty-one years.

Whatever your story, the key lesson is to find strength in those around you at times of your own weakness. Despair will suffocate you. Love and hope will empower you.

FOREWORD
BY IRMA KURTZ

To fall in love is one side-effect of being human. Falling in love can be a blessing, and it can be a disaster. We all know cases when the blaze of blinding light generated by the fall into love subsides into lifelong warmth between a pair of partners. But as often as not, we all know for ourselves that the fall into love happening as it almost always does by accident on what one writer in the collection calls *"A Rough Road"* can leave its victim with a broken heart in the debris of shattered hope. *Love Unboxed* is a collection of true stories that are every bit as engaging as fiction tries to be when it deals with the topic of love. The stories are told by women, each of whom endured at least one serious fall into love before finally emerging from her recuperation with hope restored by wisdom and a mended heart that is happier than ever before. Although each writer tells us how she managed to climb up out of the chasm and stand in sunshine again, referring to this work as an "advice manual" would denigrate the special tones of the essayists and the music of their voices in chorus. One point of interest, too, is that the harmony of these tales arises from the voices of women who live in various parts of the big world, including those where ancient traditions and parental controls are geared to prevent girls falling into love that has not been prearranged by their elders. The stories span age groups too, thus more than one of them reminisces on maternal love which is, after all, the result of sexual love and remains a version of love to be felt only by females.

Love Unboxed is about love, yes, and it is also a work of love that wants its readers to benefit. Being more than just a good read, the collection offers an important revelation with which every tale in its own way concludes: falling in love delivers a woman into the partnership which she believes deep down to be the one that she deserves. And so, these tales are presented in evidence that for a woman to find herself falling out of love with a disappointing or abusive partner is often as not the result of low self-esteem that made her fall for him in the first place. *"Dreams are Made of Love"* is the title of one in this collection of stories. And does it not also go without saying that love is made of dreams? No two human beings ever dream precisely the same dreams. Each of us makes her own dreams deriving from a part of herself which is all too often shut back into darkness as soon as she is awake again. But feeling and thinking can be joined within one person, and only when that happens will her dreams be seen and achievable, too, by daylight. Thus, do the tales in *Love Unboxed* illustrate that for a woman's meeting with Mister Wonderful to be a blessing, she needs first to meet herself. And before a partner can hold her in respectful affection she must first respect herself. And for the love of another to be the hoped-for voyage of joyful discovery, the first person a woman should love is herself.

-" Irma Kurtz, Author, Journalist, Self-help writer. Best known for her column as Agony Aunt at Cosmopolitan for over 40 years.

TABLE OF CONTENTS

Foreword by Irma Kurtz ix

Introduction xv

Part One: Passion, Romance, Fairy Tale 1

1. Placida Acheru – 20 Courageous Women 2

2. Arantxa De Dios – My First Love 6

3. Olga Frankow – Finding my Beautiful Relationship 21

4. Moni Rodriguez – Dreams Are Made of Love 33

5. Gema Ramírez – True Love Road 44

Part Two: Self Discovery, Self-Love and Hope 60

1. Omowunmi Olunloyo – A rough road 61

2. Dina Marais – Ditching the Victim in Me 73

3. Prem Glidden – Falling in Love ... with Me 88

4. Michelle Catanach – From Lost Soul to Living a
   Life Less Caged 100

5. Joh Johnson – A Melody of Sorts 115

Part Three: Patience, Survival and Broken Dreams.................................**130**

1. Kim M. Lovegrove – Killing Me Softly with His Song................................131

2. Caroline Newman – A Stepmother's Tale........................143

3. Julia Keller – My Authentic Love Story...........................158

4. Cherron Lee Johnson – A Symbolic Reflection.............171

5. Toni Harris Taylor – Drastic Steps for Love..................184

Part Four: Abuse, Pain, Fear and Freedom......................**196**

1. Evakarin Wallin – The Answer Lies Within Us............197

2. Laura Buxó – How I Met My Husband..............................209

3. Gloria Boma Alabo – Melancholy Love...........................222

4. JayJay Williams – Breaking the Cycle..............................245

Catherine Palmer – How to Create the Ideal Relationship...................................**261**

Conclusion....................................**266**

About the Publisher....................................**268**

Book Projects....................................**270**

INTRODUCTION

"When we do the best, we can, we never know what miracle is wrought in our life, or in the life of another."

– Helen Keller

This book is about women who appear from the outside to have the perfect lives, but when you look a little further you find that is far from the truth. The journey that life has taken them is far from being straight forward and smooth. In many cases, it is full of heartache, misery and torture. Hurt can be both mental and physical. It can be delivered instantly or continuously.

If you touch a hot surface, the sudden jolt of pain pulls your hand away fast to minimise the damage caused. This is not the case if the surface is warm and the heat is turned up slowly. Before you know it, your skin is sticking to the hot surface and you cannot pull away without leaving some of yourself behind. This is like the toxic relationships in which some women have found themselves trapped. They desperately want to leave, but part of them is stuck there and they cannot pull away. The longer they wait the worse it gets, and the damage caused to them just gets worse. Eventually they accept the damage as the pain is too intense and they have no choice to pull away or they will die.

The title of this book is *Love Unboxed*. I have not mentioned the feeling of "Love" yet. Love is the passion that the twenty women that have contributed to this book have for other women. It has taken real bravery for them to open their hearts and souls to publish their "real" stories behind the make-up, broad smiles and their corporate name tags.

"Learn to enjoy every minute of your life. Be happy now. Don't wait for something outside of yourself to make you happy in the future. Think how precious is the time you should spend, whether it's at work or with your family. Every minute should be enjoyed and savored."

~ Earl Nightingale

PART ONE

PASSION,
ROMANCE,
FAIRY TALE

20 COURAGEOUS WOMEN
Placida Acheru: London

*"It took me quite a long time to develop a voice,
and now that I have it, I am not going
to be silent."*

~ Madeleine Albright

I have wanted to commission a book about women for many years. This I hope is not my last, but the first of many. Women need a voice. I believe in the collaboration of hearts and souls to help other women rise and be their best self. It is a book to say you are not alone. You have strength. I hope this book helps you find that passion inside, to find the real you and to see it bloom.

Many decisions in life are made in a split second because they seem the best choice at the time. From the stories these amazing women have shared, there is a common theme that each knew in the back of their minds that this was not the correct decision to make, yet in every case, we all walked straight in front of that speeding truck. In a few cases, the choice to walk in front of that speeding truck was a cry for help, a scream to be heard or an action to get noticed. In each case, we failed to use our intuition, our inner strength and to make the right decision and stop to let the speeding truck pass by.

It is not my intention to dwell of how difficult it is to recover from being hit by a speeding truck, but I know from my own story that it can take quite some time. I have been fortunate and my prayers have been answered and somebody, an English man, who against all the odds grabbed me literally by the hand, pulled me back (originally against my will) and has not let go ever since.

As a child and growing up, I always thought I would meet one person, get married, have kids and grow old with that one person. I was going to lead a fairy tale life of knights, castles and rose gardens. Life's plan had a different story for me. It took me on a path were the words, "I love you" started to have no meaning. When I heard the words, the substance and real meaning behind them was missing. It had reached the point that I started to feel that I was the problem. We always start to feel it is the woman's fault. It is our failure.

You might wonder why a person who is branded as a "Business Coach" is compiling a book about Love! I was motivated by my hurting deep inside. I am a Top Business Transformation Coach, 3x Bestselling Author, Founder, Mentor, Digital Strategist, the list goes on. With all the business tags, I had no love in my life. I was working hard building my business, putting myself out there to attract clients, enjoying the buzz and excitement of being out there talking to people, helping, then going home alone, to an empty flat. No one to share my day with. No one to keep me warm at night. I was helping develop people. Helping them find strength, but completely neglecting myself. I had been hurt and abandoned too often to look for love anymore. It was not welcome in my life, but by giving up on it, I was in fact giving up on me. I am writing this book because I found the strength to accept love. I always will. I want to help others find it too. The best way I feel I can do that is to show you other women and prove you are not alone. It will happen if you visualise it enough and do not give up on yourself.

You will see that in each of these stories each woman had to find a love of "themselves" first. By starting to love yourself, you will find that you begin attracting love into your own life. I am not staying it is easy. You need to find the space to take a step back from the pressures you are under that are suppressing this love. And once you do, make loving yourself the priority.

I pray that you find strength within the pages of this book. Each story has its own power and will resonate differently with different people. The one that is in tune with you will be your story, your strength. It will be your redemption and the rope that will help you climb out of your predicament and find love of yourself.

The contributing authors are women from diverse races and cultures. We have done our best not to take away the uniqueness of their voice and writing. Open your mind, read, enjoy. My one request to you is, support these women by leaving a review on amazon, it would mean a lot to them. Thank you.

MY FIRST LOVE
Arantxa De Dios: London

*Let us always meet each other with a smile, for
the smile is the beginning of love.*

~ Mother Teresa

I remember it very clearly, even now, twenty years later. The first time I fell in love. It was late in my eighteenth year and, as well as being in many respects a typical girl of that age, I was suffering from anxiety due to losing two people who were close to me in the same year. I met a guy who was also suffering from anxiety. In my vulnerable state, I felt he was the only person who could understand me, who knew what it meant to feel like you could almost die every time you had a panic attack. We immediately and strongly connected through our shared anxiety.

This was my first love. When I first loved with everything I had, when I first felt butterflies in my stomach, when I first felt that being far away from someone was almost too painful to take, and when I first allowed someone to love me in return. I opened my heart completely, without boundaries and without thought. I was young. It was cool to have a boyfriend, everybody else had one. And now I did too, I was sure that it would last forever.

It lasted two and half years, fortunately no longer than that. The story of this relationship was so extreme, full of impulsivity, a rollercoaster of emotional ups and downs, too often with tears of hurt (my tears), and as time went by fewer and fewer smiles. I went from one extreme to another. My love became hate. I found myself trapped in the web of manipulation of a man who I'd discovered was a hugely toxic person. I was going around in circles, desperately trying to find the exit, but I couldn't get out. I didn't know how. I didn't feel strong enough. I was vulnerable and anxious, far worse than before. My self-esteem was almost zero. I felt empty, that I was nothing. I felt like he had taken everything from inside me, my heart and soul, my identity, my very being. I was so fragile. I was like a porcelain doll, broken in a thousand pieces. I was low, in a very dark place.

I wanted to escape it all. It consumed my thoughts. And, bit by bit, I started to emotionally free myself. I started to dream about a different life, and the dreams became more focused. I started to explore a number of different options. Finally, I could see an alternative life for myself and made my decision. I decided to not only leave this toxic person. I left everything. Yes, absolutely everything. My family, my home, my friends, my city, my country, my studies. Everything. I left. I had one suitcase and 50.000 pesetas. I was alone, although not completely. I was with my dream. With my excitement. With my vulnerability. With my pain. With my fear. With my love for my family and friends. With a tiny ray of light and of happiness. And, most importantly, with my freedom.

LEAVING ON A JET PLANE

I can still feel now the feeling I had in my stomach when my plane took off from Madrid airport. Every muscle in my body was tight, and tears streamed down my face. I looked out of the window, closed my eyes and said to myself, "Dad, Mum, Sara (my sister) I love you." And then I was gone, on my way to I didn't know what in Paris.

The feeling I had when I landed is one that we've all experienced at least once in our lives. When everything around you is brand new, and it makes you feel like you're a child again, with your childlike astonishment at it all, the ability to absorb everything you see and hear, and the desire not to miss a thing.

It was a new start. It was a new chapter of my life. And I was ready for it.

PARIS ... THE CITY OF LOVE?

However, certain aspects of my old life wouldn't disappear easily. It took me almost one more year to close the door completely to my ex-boyfriend, who was still destructive and obsessed with controlling me. He didn't make it easy for me, but he didn't succeed, because I had become stronger. I had started to love myself again. I remember the last time he called me. I was at my office in Paris and I told him to delete my number and never call me again. I hung up. I felt light and peaceful. And this time, he never called back.

My first love experience taught me some hard but important lessons, and I promised myself to never allow someone to treat me like that, and to never allow myself to suffer so much. I learnt the importance of putting boundaries on what was and wasn't acceptable behaviour, and to put my own wellbeing as my priority.

During my two first years in Paris I didn't want a serious relationship. I needed time to recover and rediscover myself, to reach the position where I could love someone else again. Eventually, I began my second relationship, one that was to last 8 years. However, my previous experience had left a mark on me. I woke up many nights and stared at my new boyfriend for hours asking myself "will he hurt me too?" Fortunately, he never did. Unfortunately, although we had a very good level of communication, our relationship was missing something that I needed; the little things that fuel a relationship. Holding hands, loving touches, or putting arms around each other. The warm and tender words, that special look only a couple in love can share. I realised that I was holding back, controlling my feelings. I didn't want to open up completely, in fact I just couldn't, because I was still scared after my first experience. I was protecting my heart. The fact that my boyfriend was naturally quite cold himself only helped me, and our relationship, to remain that way.

The years passed and I started to believe more and more in myself. I started to be warmer. I realised that I was ready to show all my feelings again, to feel loved, properly loved, with the same romance that all of us dream of. However, when I tried to grab his hand, he rejected it. He wasn't interested in real romance, and he wouldn't change. We carried on like that for years. We could talk for hours about a million different subjects; however, we couldn't talk for a minute about building our dreams and future together. We were companions, friends only in a relationship because we were in our comfort zone. But it seemed easier to stay like this than to split up.

SOME GAPS ARE JUST TOO WIDE

The fifteen-year age gap between us didn't help. At the beginning, I couldn't see the difference. It happened with time. We just didn't fancy doing the same things. I was still young I wanted to see the world, to explore, to learn. But he was settled in his life, the life he'd had for years. We repeated the same activities, with the same people. The weekends were like rituals. And still he didn't once spoil me or make me feel like a princess. Here I was again, in a relationship where I didn't like where I was but didn't know where I wanted to go. But I knew that I was bored. And when I'm bored I'm unhappy.

So, I decided to leave Paris and move back to Spain (although not my hometown). My boyfriend followed me, and soon afterwards we moved to a small island in the Balearics. At the beginning, we were surrounded and distracted by the novelty of a completely different and unique lifestyle. However, the romance was still missing. I was still trying, and he was still rejecting my efforts. Angry and upset, after a while I too started to stop trying.

One summer night, I was in a restaurant by the beach and I sensed other men looking at me. I had never noticed it before. But I noticed it then. And, to be honest, I liked it. It made me feel alive and special. And at the same time extremely sad. I believe that when you are with the right person you have a bubble around you that keeps the two of you totally focused on each other. Don't get me wrong, I'm not blind and even now sometimes I notice other men looking at me. However, although it puts a momentary little smile on my face (who doesn't like to feel attractive!), it is in no way important to me.

After that night, I had the same question in my head for months: "Do I love him?" To hear these words inside me brought both sadness and fear.

I kept it a secret until one day, after a few mojitos with one of my best friends, I told her. Just voicing these doubts had an immediate impact on me. If I was asking myself this question, I knew deep down that meant that the love was already gone. Indeed, it was. I found the courage to stop the relationship soon after, telling him with as much kindness as I could that I didn't love him anymore. It was clear in my mind that I wanted to make a clean break, to avoid any risk of having an affair or cheating on him. Most importantly, I didn't need to have someone else waiting for me to leave him. I was happy with me. I was strong enough to leave him after almost a decade together. I was ready to make another change, and this time I wasn't running away from anything.

LONDON... FULL OF ADVENTURE, OF POSSIBILITIES... BUT OF LOVE?

I left the island and moved to London, following my new dream to become fluent in English and start a business there. I was happily single, and spent a lot of time considering what I really wanted in both my professional and personal life. I hoped that London was not only the right place to start a new career but also, just maybe, to start the most beautiful love story of my life.

After being single for couple of years, I again needed to love and to be loved. I was fed up of being chatted up by guys who were prepared to cheat on their partners. It seemed that everybody was in a relationship, and that all the good men were taken. I admit that I was jealous when I saw happy couples together. I wanted to fall in love like them. I wanted a man who would hold my hand and never let it go, who would be crazy about me and I would be crazy about him. I was looking around, I was meeting new people, I even tried online dating once, however I couldn't find somebody who ticked all my boxes. My expectations were high. After my previous experiences, I was very selective. I wanted to find Mr Right, the man of my life. I was already thirty-four years old and I didn't want to waste my time on casual encounters or relationships which would never go anywhere. My biological clock was ticking, although I wasn't in a rush. I always believed that one day I would be a mum, but at the same time I was very clear in my mind that my children must be a product of real and unconditional love.

It happened one day in November. I was on my way to meet a new client I would teach French one-to-one. I was sitting in the reception of his office, waiting for him. I heard a male voice say my name. I looked up and saw him in front of me. I remember my instant reaction; OMG he is hot!! He said "Hi, I'm James."

During our first lesson, I discovered that James was in a relationship, as he was using 'we' a lot. I was disappointed and thought to myself, that's one more that got away. We carried on with our lessons for months. We got on well. Extremely well. Without having to try. It was so natural. There was something between us, a connection, a chemistry, we both sensed it even at an early stage. We started to talk about our personal stuff as part of the lessons, which were more about conversation than textbooks. We learnt more about each other. James was curious about my life. The summer arrived and we started to have lessons in the park and then in a bar. The lessons lasted longer, instead of one hour they became two and sometimes two and a half. James always complained when he was leaving that he couldn't believe the lesson went so quickly and would have loved to stay longer. After every lesson, James would text me to say thanks and how much he enjoyed it. Sometimes he sent me a message just to say good night. On his birthday, James brought me a cake he'd saved from work. I was thinking to myself "How sweet, and how weird! None of my others clients are doing this. What does it mean?"

I began to realise that I was really attracted to this guy. I could feel that something not only existed between us, but that it was growing. However, I never forgot that James wasn't single. It was clear to me that I wouldn't have an 'adventure' with him. It was also clear that I was ready, I wanted, to have a serious relationship with him. I felt huge frustration.

I was falling in love with someone who wasn't free and seemingly wasn't going to be free. I decided to prioritise my wellbeing and stop the classes with James. I told him; he wasn't happy but accepted it. I remember that, as we said goodbye and I was going up the escalator to my train, I looked down and saw James looking up at me, with sadness written all over his face. My stomach was tight. I was sad too, for days and days. I felt that something was wrong in my decision. I thought about it again and again, and arrived at the conclusion that I needed to change my mind, to continue with the lessons. I wanted to test the strength of the feelings between us. I also missed being with James, and him being a part of my life. He was my favourite student! So, I contacted him again and we restarted the lessons, keeping our distance slightly, pretending we were comfortable being just friendly, and hiding our true feelings.

EMBRACING SADNESS AND VULNERABILITY TO BECOME STRONGER

One day my mum called me saying that my dad had a serious heart situation and needed a major operation which carried serious risks. I went back to Spain immediately, not knowing when I would be back. I stayed there for almost 4 weeks. James was incredibly supportive. He was sending me three or four emails per day asking for news about the situation and how I was. One day we had a lesson on

Skype and James told me that he had a strong feeling of wanting to be next to me in this difficult moment. At the end of the lesson, and I don't know why or how I did this, but I told him that I was missing him a lot. James answered; "me too."

During the period of my Dad's illness, I was very emotional and vulnerable. It was a strange irony to me that as his heart was struggling badly, mine was pumping more strongly than ever. During those four weeks in Spain, being with my family in an environment reminding me that life is short and to be lived, I had time to reflect to myself about what I really wanted from James in my life. I found the courage to send him an email written with all my heart and soul. I told him how strong my feelings for him were, and how hard it was for me knowing that we couldn't be together. I had taken off the mask I had been wearing with him, and it led to an amazing reaction from James. He answered back almost immediately doing exactly the same. He told me how he was struggling with his intense feelings for me, how he sensed the chemistry and connection that refused to go away, the sleepless nights he had been having for weeks asking himself many of the same questions I was asking myself. We had now opened up; we knew that we felt the same way, that we were 'in the same boat'; but, we still didn't know what - if anything - to do about it. What we did know is that we needed to talk, badly.

Thankfully my Dad's heart operation was a success and he was soon out of hospital. I had to get back to my life. As soon as I came back to London, James and I met for our weekly lesson, except this time it would be very different. We had the most honest conversation I have ever had. We put our cards on the table, revealing our entire personalities, our faults, what we loved and hated, the skeletons in our closets, and most importantly the non-negotiable things that we wanted in life and a relationship. It was incredible to discover how all our cards matched! We knew at that moment that we were meant to be with each other.

Things moved very fast. James and I became a couple immediately. After one month, we were living together. After three months, we were pregnant. 10 months after our daughter was born we were married, and today after 4 years together we are expecting a baby boy. All my painful, sad and frustrating previous relationship experiences eventually led me to the right man, in the right place, and at the right time. I couldn't wish for a better relationship, and every day is special.

So what did I learn from my relationship experience over 20 years? I learnt that for whatever you want in life, you need speak with your heart; you need be totally and utterly and unapologetically you; you need show what's in your mind and soul. Don't be ashamed of your vulnerability (it's very sexy!), or hide behind this mask that we all put on sometimes. Understanding on a fundamental level who you are, what you want, what you like and don't like, and what your non-negotiables are, right now is key to being able to communicate that and find those who match you. Visualise your life as you want it to be. Dream about it. Your thoughts are the most powerful thing you have. Believe in your ability to make your dream a reality. Prioritise your love for yourself - as you are - part of which is being honest with yourself on the areas where you could and should improve. If you respect yourself, the rest of the world will respect you. If you love yourself, the rest of the world (or at least those worthy of you) will love you. Above all, just be that beautiful and unique person that you are.

ABOUT THE AUTHOR

Arantxa combines a life coaching qualification with her multilingualism and natural energy to coach people in any one of 4 languages to find balance, make important decisions and transform their lives. As someone who has lived a colourful and varied life in several countries, and has been coached substantially herself, Arantxa brings real world experience and knows how to put herself in the shoes of her clients to provide them with maximum value. Arantxa specialises in coaching on all things to do with relationships, as well as becoming a parent and relocation and expatriation among many other important life themes.

CONTACT:

http://www.arantxadedios.com

FINDING MY BEAUTIFUL
RELATIONSHIP
Olga Frankow: London

*"Love is friendship that has caught fire. It
is quiet understanding, mutual confidence,
sharing and forgiving. It is loyalty through good
and bad times. It settles for less than perfection
and makes allowances for human weaknesses."*

~ Ann Landers

Before becoming a relationship coach, I had a long story of failures in intimate relationships, and there was definitely a point when I didn't believe in an emotionally fulfilling and committed relationship. I have gone from believing that first love has to stay with you forever to the idea you have to go through a few divorces before you can actually find a person you can truly connect and spend the rest of your life with. The extreme limits of my beliefs kept changing depending on the environment I was in. But to understand why I became who I am now, I need to start from the beginning.

At school I used to be a what they call "cute" girl. I had a lot of attention from boys from the early age. I have to admit I enjoyed it and never questioned it, I was sure it was due to me being such nice girl. And my family kept reassuring me about it, so I created a strong belief in my own invulnerability. I developed it into something close to a "princess" mode, and kept playing boys, never taking any of them seriously as I was sure one day I would meet my prince charming and we will live happily ever after! And he didn't have to wait too long.

At the age of fourteen, I was madly in love! And he was of course a prince, in his own way, but also a sixteen-year-old school drop-out, drug-addict, who I thought, represented all possible masculine qualities you need in a man, and who cares that he would probably never go to college or have any real career. I was dreaming about marrying him one day and have lots of babies together!

Still only a teenager! Not bad for the start to my love-life. We were together for two years of my high school. But "together" is a way too strong word for describing that relationship. In reality, it was him showing up at my door-step whenever it was comfortable for him. He disappeared for weeks, either drinking or smoking weed and obviously never bothered telling me he was still alive. Mind you, it was the era before mobile phones! So I had no idea if I'd ever see him again after such breaks. Meanwhile, I spent my nights crying, filling in my diary with sad thoughts, and arguing with my mom that he was the best guy in the world and I would do anything to make it work! After all, this is what we girls are supposed to do.

We believe we need to take care of our men, bearing any pain they cause us and carry on loving them for who they are and be happy they've chosen us to be their women! Looking back from my current grown-up position, I can probably understand why I behaved that way at the time. My parents got divorced when I was nine, and all I remember about their relationship was arguing and disappointment. That's why at that tender age I accepted the idea that love comes with pain and it is perfectly normal to be with someone who causes you pain, but if you stick around long enough, you can eventually be happy! Maybe some of you can recognise yourselves in this scenario.

Sadly, it is not uncommon. And as much as our family tries to protect us, we seem to be able to learn only by our mistakes. And that was exactly what I did, one by one I learned from unsuccessful relationships until one day I not only met the man of my dreams, but also realised the amount of work and commitment that are required to be in a happy relationship.

NO MORE LOVE TRAPS

After my first love left me heart-broken, I declared to myself I would never fall into the love trap again. And I didn't, but not only because I wanted it, but also because guys stopped being attracted to me all together. After school I moved from a small town to a new, unknown world of a big city where I went to university. It was a very exciting time, meeting so many new people, learning so many new things, not only about mathematics, which was my master subject, but also about life in general. Here I realised that all my looks, which were so popular back in my town, faced a big competition with beautiful girls of a big city!

Although, now I strongly believe – it is not only the looks that attract men in women, but back then, it ruined my little "princes" bubble that I had lived in for so many years. My self-esteem went down to an almost zero level. In addition, I started putting on weight, living on a student's diet consisting mainly of pizza and pasta, which was not helping either. By year three in university, I was sure I would die alone and no one would ever love me again. It did hurt tremendously to say the least. Added to that was the family pressure that you must find a life partner in university, otherwise when you start working your chances only go down from there.

WHERE WOULD I SEEK ADVICE?

There was no one to help me understand my concerns. This is not something we learn in school. Now I realised I must have been not the only one feeling that way. A lot of girls at such vulnerable age, seek a proof of their lovability outside of themselves, having so little self-love and instead being highly self-judgemental. It seems to them that no one could understand them, therefore they choose to stay one-on-one with their struggles and insecurities. I was not an exception, I kept pushing myself to lose weight, because I imagined when I am slim enough, he, the ONE, would appear at my door step.

However, only when I gave up on all my attempts to change anything, as it often happens, I met my big love number two. He was everything I could dream of! We both instantly fell in love, from the first night we met. There was only one problem, he lived a thousand miles away! He came to my town on vacation to visit his relatives and we spent the most romantic three weeks together. We could not stay apart for a minute, let along thinking about him leaving back home.

When the time came, we had to go through the most heart-breaking good-bye scene you could only see in Hollywood movies. On a final kiss, he put something in my pocket, and told me to look at it afterwards only. It was a little hand-written message about how much he loved me, and how much we were meant to be together. It was beautiful. We promised to write letters to each other, because it was still the pre-mobile phone era. I only received one letter from him and never heard from him again. Which proves the concept that a holiday romance rarely grows into something serious.

People revert to their usual routine and responsibilities, at which point they realise they are not ready to make that much effort the love on distance requires and soon enough it becomes an only another romantic story in their history of "non-working" relationships.

Therefore, at the age of twenty, I stopped believing in true, romantic love, especially love at first sight. Without realising it at the time, I protected myself from being hurt again with a strong belief that there were no good men out there until one day a guy from my university group decided to pursue me. And to be fair to him, he did a lot to win my attention, he was taking me to movies, bringing me chocolates and was patiently waiting until I responded with at least the slightest step from my side.

It taught me a few important lessons, first of all, men can actually invest in the relationship if they want to, second, we women have to give them space to do this and not jump ready to be there for them on a first call, thirdly, falling in love can be a slow process and can happen with someone you've known for ages, but simply didn't look at them in a romantic light. It took me some time to figure out what kind of feelings I had towards this man.

I knew it was not love in its typical form when you cannot sleep, cannot eat and spend half of your time day-dreaming. And that was the only love I've known before. But this time it was different, after a few months of trying to ignore him, I gave in and decided to give it a go. My mom and grandma considered him a very good catch and were very happy that I finally settled, because it was only one year to go before the graduation and my clock was ticking. Here we were, moving in together after a few months, constantly fighting, but I accepted it as normal. After all, all couples fight, and there is nothing we can do about it.

Only when I learnt everything I know about relationships today, I realised that I wasn't in a healthy place to build a strong bond with someone, I didn't love myself, in fact I was sure I was the worst walking example of love disasters, therefore I didn't deserve to have a perfect love story, and "prince charming" would never exist in my own story.

My relationship with this man started falling apart, as after graduation we moved to a new city, faced a lot more challenges than existed in a student life, and I realised I was conquering the world on my own. I had ambitions and plans, I wanted to change and grow, learn more and excel in my career while all he wanted was to chill out. He was expecting me to be in the driving seat and drag him after me wherever I would decide we should go.

I was working longer hours than he, and was expected to all the household chores afterwards, simply because I am a woman and this is what women do. And it is me who wanted the house and the dishes clean, therefore I should do the cleaning, because he was perfectly fine with a pile of unwashed dishes and a layer of dust on the floor. Of course, a lot of couples argue about these things and it is not a reason for a break-up. The real reason lies in the background.

When you realise you cannot rely on someone that close to you, when he doesn't support you in any of your challenges, it means he simply doesn't meet your basic needs in a relationship. In the last two years of our life together, I read a great amount of self-development books, and I changed a lot. My level of self-awareness significantly increased, I learnt to love and respect myself and finally re-found that long time lost self-value. While my man preferred to stay comfortably where he was, and not follow me. He just didn't have the need to change, and I don't blame him. It was his conscious choice, and there is nothing wrong with it. I could only regret that I did not learn sooner about myself and what I wanted in life. We were simply incompatible in too many ways, therefore that relationship just couldn't work.

Learning from yet another mistake, I realised, you not only need to find someone compatible with you, but also someone with whom you can go in the same direction with. Someone who is sharing your values, be it for growth, or exploration, or success, you need to know that he will be there for you no matter what you decide to do. And I am not saying you have to agree on absolutely everything, but you wouldn't go far without agreeing on fundamental values of life.

EIGHTEEN MONTHS OF LOVE OVER THE INTERNET

When I met my now husband Rafael, I instantly could see the difference in my behaviour around him. I was no longer needy and scared girl who was looking for someone's approval of her self-worth, but a confident woman, emotionally fulfilled and sure of what she wanted in life. I was ready to share my life with someone who deserves to be with me, and I would not compromise on any of my standards.

We met on vacation and spent only one night together before going back to our home countries, miles away from each other. Given my previous experience, I didn't believe in "distant" love, but my future husband proved me wrong, and I am glad he did. We were exchanging a hundred emails per day, talking all night long on Skype (luckily it already existed at the time!). And he travelled to visit me in Ukraine, he organised our holiday together, then he arranged his work so he could work from home, and spent a few months with me in Ukraine. He showed he would do anything for us to be together.

This was the difference to all my previous relationships. By then I knew, your man has to be willing to invest his share into the relationship and you don't have to go an extra mile for him. You should meet halfway, then you can build a healthy committed relationship. So we did, after 1.5 years of love via Internet, we moved in together in Poland and later moved to the UK, where we got married. Of course, there were a lot of ups and downs in our relationship too. But what made a huge difference is our wiliness to work on ourselves.

We both have an open-minded approach to life, we are eager to learn and improve, which are the most important traits in a relationship development. We have a vision not only for our individual lives and careers, but for us as a couple, sharing our dreams, ambitions and aspirations. This allowed us to create such a strong connection and high level of trust, that even when we do argue, we are able to recover from it very quickly and return to a positive state.

MY RELATIONSHIP LESSON

The biggest lesson we learnt about our relationship over the years is that you have to be willing to be your best self for your partner, and be aware of their needs, focusing on giving rather than receiving. It has worked very well for us for almost eight years now. That's why I decided to become a relationship coach and share our experience with other couples. And I am not saying we have it all figured out, I think it is always work in progress. But as long as we enjoy this journey together, we stay happy and fulfilled.

ABOUT THE AUTHOR

Olga is a highly skilled Relationship Coach, qualified by Animas coaching school and accredited by Coaching Standards Authority. She works with couples and singles to achieve their ultimate relationship goals and enjoy happier lives with their loved ones. Olga's coaching complies with highest standards of integrity, confidentiality and quality of service.

CONTACT:

http://www.olgafrankow.com

DREAMS ARE MADE OF LOVE
Moni Rodriguez: London

"One's philosophy is not best expressed in words; it is expressed in the choices one makes... and the choices we make are ultimately our responsibility."

~ Eleanor Roosevelt

I am a dreamer. A reflective, crazy dreamer! I believe in love. I believe in passion. I believe in seizing the day (and the night!), being next to the people I love the most. To me, love should make you feel in constant awe of a person, feeling joy inside, feeling that life has meaning and purpose. And I have always believed that dreams do come true - if you take risks and if you don't get weighed down with your fears. First of all, you must commit to loving yourself. Perhaps that's why I love this quote so much.

"It's the possibility of having a dream come true that makes life interesting. " Paulo Coelho

I don't know about you, but I enjoy making my life as interesting as possible. So, when my ex and I decided to divorce, I knew there was something more powerful waiting for me. I knew that it was the right decision. Staying together just didn't feel right. The relationship didn't feel full of passion, love or joy anymore. Totally the opposite! So it was destined to end.

MOM, I AM GETTING DIVORCED

I still remember the day I told my parents I was getting divorced. They were shocked. For our families, the most shocking thing of all was the way in which we communicated the news that we were separating. We were calm and happy with our decision to divorce. Not much drama or a protracted 'blaming' game. We were smiling. We did it together. We somehow understood that separating was part of the process to becoming better people. Yes, there was pain - the pain of breaking family relationships and of not meeting the expectations of everyone. I felt like a failure. I desperately didn't want to disappoint others. The perfect daughter that never gets anything wrong had messed up!

After just one year of marriage, we decided to separate.

After communicating that I was getting divorced, some people in my close environment were quick to tell me, "I knew it wouldn't last!" I was quite surprised. After all, what did other people know about my intimate and private life? Judgement can come quickly when people aren't particularly happy with their own lives.

It was a big lesson for me. So my message to you is to watch carefully those who are in and around your life. Always. Invest your time and energy with only people who lift you up. Forget the rest. Life is too short.

One year before our divorce, my ex and I embarked on a transformational journey. We didn't know the extent of that transformation, but it was more than I ever thought it would be. We left everything behind, the well-paid jobs, family and friends and a recently purchased home.

We put our flat up for rent, packed a few boxes and quit our jobs. We needed to start all over again in Ireland. After seven years of being in a relationship and two years of living together, he wanted adventure, and I was up for it as well. People thought we were crazy. Deep inside something inside my heart was telling me that this move would bring us closer or it would be the end. As you already know, for us, it became the end of our story together and the beginning of an incredible personal journey for me.

What did I learn from it? Well, getting used to someone is easy. In the beginning, you are really in love, and that person feels perfect for you. However, once you start sharing your life, if you haven't healed your emotional wounds or you do not know who you truly are, problems are inevitable. Expectations are not met and fall short. Once I was out of my comfort zone and my emotional support circle was miles away from me, I started questioning many things. I felt terribly lonely when we moved to Ireland. This feeling was not a new one. Shortly after moving, I realised that I have felt alone all my life.

I had spent seven years of my life with someone and it had become more of a friendship than a love relationship. I didn't want to settle. I believe no one should. I knew first and foremost that I needed to get to know myself better and to make self-love a priority in my life.

MY LITTLE GIRL

Every woman has a little girl inside wanting to be loved and protected. Dreaming to live and discover true love.

When I was a little girl, I loved Jane Austen stories. I would create theatre scenes in my room. I would imagine that I had met my Mr. Darcy. I would create my own scenes of "Pride and Prejudice", fantasising with the idea that our love would be an eternal romance that would last until the end of our days.

When I was fifteen, a guy who I had liked a lot since the age of twelve, asked me out. I was in heaven. But then fear started to creep in. Shortly afterwards, I understood that I was too young and immature even to consider a relationship.

Two weeks later, I left the guy without even having given him my first kiss.

I decided to forget about love for a while and focus on my studies. No more 'little girl dreams' allowed.

I do wonder when the story changed. I wonder what happened to that little girl. For years, I moved away from my dream world to a world of new expectations. These were mostly about fulfilling other people's expectations. I was seeking their approval all the time.

As a teen, I fell in love several times with guys who completely ignored me or ultimately broke my heart. During my twenties, I found myself with a cold heart, not caring if the guys were interested in me or not. I was living in my fantasy world, just looking to be happy at any cost.

No more broken hearts allowed. However, deep inside, I was ready to love anyone who showed some interest in me. Trying to escape that place of 'not being lonely', I ended up on some occasions making the wrong choices.

I spent my twenties trying to seek the approval of the men who I shared my life with. At work, I became a woman with a male persona, looking for something outside of myself without knowing why I had this need to feel 'loved and saved' all the time.

At the end of my twenties, I had many people around me and was in a long-term relationship and yet I was feeling lonely inside. For years, I ignored the call from within my heart. I was too busy attempting to live what everyone would call a 'normal' life.

Doing my best to fulfil everyone's expectations about what I was 'supposed' to be doing, I finally looked to my heart. I started to believe that perhaps true love doesn't exist and that my Mr. Darcy only existed in my dreams.

After our separation, I began living alone. My heart was ready to explore what real love is and was prepared to get to know who on earth I was. Those 'little girl dreams' started to come alive again.

TRUE LOVE

I was lonely and sad trying to figure out who I truly was and feeling that something was totally wrong. Days were passing by and each day on my way to work I would cry. Rainy days, sad days. The only thing I wanted was to meet my true soulmate. I started to believe that the love I had dreamed about as a girl was possible. One sunny day, on Saint Patrick's Day to be exact, it happened!

I met him at work. He lived far away from me, 5,200 miles to be exact. He was in India and I was in Dublin. The first day we chatted was as if we had known each other for years. For months, we talked about our lives and work, our dreams and our feelings. We became virtual friends.

I never thought that I could find someone so similar to me, especially someone who was from a different background. It was strange and magnetic. He was the first person to make me feel complete. I felt he truly listened to me. For the first time, I was not feeling lonely. I felt I was cared for; no matter how many miles were between us.

After months of talking via the Internet, we knew that we couldn't forget about each other. Finally, after a year, we decided to meet in person. At that stage, we were still in the 'just friends' zone. I just couldn't believe we were finally going to meet face to face.

He travelled all the way from India to Ireland to meet me. The day we met in person was an unforgettable moment. I still remember waiting for him in the hotel hall, drinking a glass of red wine, really nervous and wondering if all that we felt during that long time of waiting to meet in person was true or not. I didn't know what to expect.

At 12:30 pm, he came down from his hotel room with a beautiful bouquet of flowers and sat in front of me. For the first few minutes, we couldn't believe that we were together in person. We had two weeks with each other, which was an incredible time travelling across the country and sharing time together.

To cut a long story short, after a year of flying back and forth to meet each other, we decided to marry. Yes, in an act of complete faith, I married him and we decided to start a life together. I applied for a role in London, got the job and he left everything behind to be with me.

Fast forward five years and we are still in love having lots of fun and sharing things together. What I have come to understand about marriage is that it is something that you need to nourish on a daily basis. The fact that we spoke for hours almost every day for more than a year before meeting face to face made us get to know each other from the inside out. A long-term relationship requires a lot of communication, understanding and particularly you need to know yourself and the other person really well. Acceptance is crucial because with time passion can fade unless you light up the fire on a daily basis.

I understood that taking some time to live alone and reflect about myself and my true desires helped me to get to know who I truly was and what I wanted from a relationship. I spent hours reading self-development books, but ultimately what helped me the most was when I decided to take care of myself without expecting anyone else to do it for me. I wholeheartedly believe that self-respect and self-love are something that should be taught at school. If we are constantly looking for someone else to fill the void of our lack of love, we will always be looking in the wrong place.

FINAL WORDS

Love is ultimately our true calling for self-discovery. I feel that what has brought me to a place of feeling complete with my love life is the fact that I now love and accept myself. It was the journey of getting to know my 'light' and my 'shadows' and love them both that enabled me to finally find someone who could see my real beauty. A beauty that goes beyond looks. When you open your heart fully to someone and you can see his soul, it's a beautiful experience. For me, it happened this way. I needed to go miles away from my hometown to go back home, inside my heart.

May all your dreams come true and may all of your love fantasies become real. The only way to get to experience them is to first of all give that same love to yourself. Feel the pain, feel all the emotions and let go of what is not necessary to you anymore. Never stop believing. Let your heart open and allow the universe to do the rest. Have faith, magic eventually happens.

ABOUT THE AUTHOR

Moni helps sensitive women to live with greater peace, passion and joy.

Currently based near London and originally from the beautiful city of Barcelona, Moni, otherwise known as Monica, believes that when women shine their light and claim their inner power, they can change the world.

With more than 15 years of experience in the corporate world, Moni has observed that a more compassionate and heart-centred leadership is required to bring back balance, equality and consciousness.

She is passionate about eliminating burnout from the corporate culture, and she is committed to supporting women led projects. Moni is helping and inspiring women around the world transform their lives and become leaders for change in both personal and professional levels.

With her writings, signature talks and support, Moni contributes to raising awareness of increasing the presence of feminine values in the world.

Moni is a certified NLP Practitioner and Energy 4 Life Wellness Coach. She is also trained in several energy-based therapies and has years of research in personal development, conscious living and spirituality.

CONTACT:

Email: info@monirodriguez.com
Website: http://www.monirodriguez.com
Instagram: https://www.instagram.com/monirodriguezsp
Facebook: https://www.facebook.com/monirodriguezsp
Twitter: https://www.twitter.com/monirodriguezsp

TRUE LOVE ROAD
Gema Ramírez: Spain

*"The best legacy we can leave the world and to
those we love is our own HAPPINESS, our own
example of a happy and fulfilled life."*

~ Gema Ramírez

ASK AND IT IS GIVEN... IN THE MOST MAGICAL WAY

I t was spring. The break of dawn found me in bed in Cádiz, the small city by the sea where I grew up. My birthday was coming up soon, so I had taken some days off to visit mum in Spain, spending time with the family.

I had been living in the UK for a few years working in a great IT job with good career prospects. A break was needed, but it wasn´t work keeping me stressed... it was my relationship. This man, whom I had a thirteen-year relationship with, had become more like a brother to me. My loving companion and friendly flat mate. There was no romantic connection left, only his persistent unrelenting need of keeping the bond going at all cost. He managed to turn my thoughts around every time I tried to break up with him. I always ended up feeling sorry for him. My catholic upbringing made me feel it was normal to sacrifice myself for his happiness. I did not know how to prioritise my needs and desires over his.

That spring morning, in my mum´s flat in Cádiz, I knew I had had enough. Lying in bed, contemplating, as I used to do in the morning, I analysed my situation.

I was only thirty-seven and the last eight years I had lived like a nun. I was faithful by nature, so going off with another man was not an option for me while

I was with him. I tried though, a few years back, I had felt this strong attraction for this Italian man at work... but I could not go through with it. So I locked myself into my imposed celibacy and devoted all my sexual energy into my career. Work gave me the most satisfaction at that point in my life.

That spring morning in Cádiz was different, however... I felt young and bustling with energy, with a whole life ahead of me and a strong wish to be in love. I so desired to enjoy my sexuality and feel wanted again.

From an uncontrollable and deeply strong desire, that spring morning I prayed to the Universe, "Please, I wish to relight my sexual relationship with PJ. I want to become one with him. I want us to be a proper couple!" Thinking about what I just shouted out, I was puzzled at the fact that I called him PJ... I had never called him by his initials before, just by his name and although I wondered what the reason may have been, I left it at that!

Two months later, after a few attempts at fixing the unfixable, I finally found the courage to break up with this man. Not only that, I was about to embark in one of many transformational personal experiences of my life. I sold my house, left my job, left my dead thirteen-year-old relationship behind. I never shed a tear or showed a sign of regret or guilt.

I moved to an adorable small cottage in the hills of Moelwyn Mawr in Tanygrisiau, in North Wales. I found the so much needed time for myself in the depths of the beautiful Snowdonia. I loved waking up to the sound of nature, looking at the sheep through my back window and waving through my front window to the tourists travelling on the historic steam train on their way towards Porthmadog. I felt so fortunate and so inspired by living there. Doing some days of consultancy IT contract work with the previous company was the perfect arrangement to get some income and have something to do.

I enjoyed my solitude. He came to visit me on a few occasions, trying to get me back. He probably truly loved me like you love someone whom you get used to having around. In fact, I realized he loved me unconditionally, but maybe it was a different kind of love, not the passionate love that I was looking for at that young age. He offered the quiet, pleasant love that one may wish to have later on in life, when things are settled, when adventures have been lived, life has been experienced, the good memories are all that are left and you are content with some company. But not now!!

I was adamant. This time I was determined and was not taking him back. It took me a few years to make the decision, but once I did it, I knew I would find the courage and the integrity to stick to it. I also knew I would be there for him until he was ready to move on, until he would be the one who would end the contact, which he did do many years later when eventually I did stop hearing from him.

On my days off work, I enjoyed driving in my MX5 convertible around the most beautiful North Wales landscapes. In the evenings, when there was only darkness and rain through my window, I would play games online to pass the time. And that's how I met him.

It was cool having this online chat to talk with the other online competitors. There was always a 'good luck' or 'good game' wish with the other players. One night, the small talk with this person hiding behind an avatar with a top hat, turned into a deeper conversation. We talked for hours, we exchanged messenger details and continued talking online until 5am in the morning. Having never done anything like it, it felt pretty exciting!

THE UNIVERSE DELIVERS THE FAIRY TALE

I found out he was an architect from the Midlands living in Paris. He had recently sold his house and moved temporarily to France to recover from the death of his father.

We were both in a similar situation, having plenty of time in our hands. We spoke in the morning again and the chatting continued for seven days in a row. On day eight, I was already driving to Liverpool airport to catch the first flight to Paris to meet him.

I had always been of an adventurous and fearless nature, now I was at it again... my intuition told me this was the right thing to do and I felt safe, not to mention exhilarated.

Arriving at Paris airport, I was so excited. My heart was pounding so hard I thought it would break through my ribs. I felt faint. For a split second as I walk through to arrivals, it occurred to me that this man may not even exist or that he may not turn up. I believed in my heart that he would, but it was only 8 days since we discovered each other and my head was twirling.

I started to write a plan B in my head... you know... just in case he was not there or there was something really wrong with him.

Online dating was a new thing back then in 2007. It had not occurred to me to say a word to anyone about my plan to visit an unknown man in Paris. At the time, I booked the flight, it sounded very unreasonable to start worrying friends and family. If I had, I do not imagine I would have had many supporters. It was so unbelievable, so irresponsible, so risky... just my type of adventure!

As I was walking out of the security and into arrivals, I thought I should have told somebody I knew what I was up to... but not out of feelings of insecurity, no, just to have someone to share with this exciting, incredible life changing moment I was about to experience.

Then WOW. He was very real. I was shocked when I saw him. He had sent me his picture only two days before my flight. I had not found him particularly attractive, but having fallen in love with his charms and personality, his looks did not matter to me.

But this man at the airport who was coming to greet me with open arms, was very attractive. He had the most beautiful smile I had ever seen. That cheeky smile that over the years became so familiar, with his little dimple on the left side that will through thick and thin kept me hooked for years.

I looked around in amazement and disbelief looking for the cameras and thinking that this was a bad joke staged by some TV program. Someone was surely just waiting to make me look stupid by jumping out of nowhere shouting 'You've been framed'!

No-one else was there though. It was just the two of us... not only was he real, he was gorgeous.

The attraction was instant for both of us. I was shaking and so was he.

We jumped into a taxi in the direction to his flat to drop my suitcase. We kissed with a passion that made me feel faint again, then off for our first walk in Paris. It was a sunny afternoon, strolling by the Seine, holding hands, kissing, laughing and smiling... it was truly breath-taking.

The next five days and nights in Paris flew by. I was living the fairy tale all women are told when we are little girls, the fairy tale that, after break ups and disillusions, we learn to dismiss as we grow older and wiser. Yet I was living it. Our love was intense. We were both in need of what we were having. He was an extremely good lover, the best I had ever had, and we complemented each other well. We drank the best French wines, ate at the best restaurants, walked in the most romantic Paris places. I knew it was MY fairy tale and I was living it to the full. Every moment, feeling each second with the wholeness of my being and recording each feeling into my heart's long term memory bank.

I was happy for the first time in a long time, I did not want this time to ever end. I experienced the fear of the uncertainty, of the uncontrollable temporariness of things, of the need to grasp with the strength of both hands those moments of extreme happiness with the raw knowingness that they will undoubtedly have an end. I wanted to be kept stuck in a time loop that repeated those five days and nights over and over. It was the most fulfilling time of my whole life.

At some point during those five days, I realized that the initials of both his names coincided with those initials I shouted out that spring morning in my mum's flat a few months back. PJ were his initials. The initials of this new man who was redefining my concept of happiness and rewriting my internal dictionary.

PJ was the same as the previous lover's name, the one who became my brother, the one I pleaded the Universe to find unity with once more. The Universe, because I only gave it the initials, had found someone else with the same letters that could actually fulfil my most intense and inner passions.

In that moment of realization, I understood that the Universe was playing along at my side, that anything I would ask for I would get. I had found the formula for wish manifestation. I learnt that I had to be more specific to obtain exactly what I wanted or expect that by asking a more general wish and leave it to the Universe's most wonderful logistic skills, the Universe would do its magic and deliver the perfect fit for the needs of the moment.

Those five days were the reasons I kept coming back to him over and over for the next seven years that, on and off, experiencing happiness and pain, we spent loving each other.

A WORLD OF MAGIC AND DUALITY

We never wanted to be apart after that first encounter in the spring of 2007. From then on, we became an item. We moved to London together, commuted to his flat in Paris, travelled to Spain, yet within all this happiness, I also found torture. The eternal duality of things is always present. I have also learnt this: having one quality in your life, like happiness, inevitably brings its opposite, and it is up to us to keep the balance with conscious awareness and choosing how we want to feel despite what's going on around us.

The man of my dreams, the object of my love and my desire, the one I wished was the ´forever saviour prince charming´ used to drive me mad with psychological abuse. I didn´t know back then I was being manipulated, mentally and emotionally, but I knew I could not take any more of the roller coaster of mixed emotions that he used to put me through.

Eventually I left him. Through the one year we were separated, I decided I needed some "casual" fun and wanted to experience a much younger man. I met this beautiful young soul who adored me and made me feel like a goddess, but in who I unfortunately didn´t find that connection.

After this failed short affair, I then decided that what I needed was a spiritual man, someone who fulfilled that strong and ever growing mystical part of me that no other man had been able to satisfy. I found out the hard way that I was very wrong, when the very spiritual man I met and moved in with, turned out to be verbally aggressive. Fearing that the verbal aggression would turn physical, I carefully planned my escape.

As I was devising the leaving strategy, PJ contacted me. He knew how to get through to me. He knew I was not happy; he could still feel me. He sent me an email with his address and asked me to come back to him, that he had changed and was still very much in love with me, that he could not have forgotten the way I walked, my smile, my face when we made love...

I did not send the email. On the day, he sent it I was busy running away from a particular hell to which I will never return. I left it all behind once and with the little money I received from the sale of my beloved Welsh cottage, where I had so many memories to be cherished forever, I decided to go back to London for two weeks and stayed with friends, before moving to Glastonbury.

The first friend I stayed with lived in South London, funnily enough, came from Tooting, near Colliers Wood, where I had lived with the original PJ during our first year of love. That evening, once settled and calmed down, I turned my computer on and found his email, that email with his address, his new phone number and his everlasting declaration of eternal love... he had returned to London, looked for a flat in Colliers Wood, the place we had lived together during our first year of love... he was hoping I would come and see him. I froze... the Universe was at play again. Following my instinct, I was staying just a few streets away from the man of my dreams. One year after I saw him for the last time, he was there, again, waiting for me, in one of the largest cities in the world. He was only five minutes from where I was staying.

And the heaven and hell story continued. After we reach out to each other again, we relived the most beautiful chapter 2, but this time in London. We separated, moved in together, separated again... the roller coaster was back in action. This time with higher peaks and more dramatic downs. I experienced the most exhilarating love and intimate connection. I experienced mind blowing sex, from sweet and romantic to deeply spiritual, from tantric and soul touching to raw and animal. I also experienced abuse, like nothing before, the type of abuse that you don´t know it´s there until years later. When you look back, you realise have never experienced being truly loved for who you are.

IF THIS ISN´T LOVE, WHAT IS?

Through all this I came to the understanding that this love was not real love, it was... yes... it was addiction. My addiction to his charming smile, his addiction to my smell, our addiction to the sexual connection, but the worse and most difficult addiction to overcome, was the addiction to the emotional roller coaster that we used to ride and to which we used to succumb because of our love for each other: That love-addiction for each other!

The story lasted a few more years during which I grew up as a woman, as a spiritual warrior, as a goddess in the making. I became wiser and stronger as I moved into my forties. I understood the nature of my love for him, the addiction and the love part. I knew one day it would inevitably be over, I had decided, because I was after real love... the love I will not want to run away from, the kind of love that will not take me into any more roller coaster rides, the love that will give me peace... the love for myself.

I came to the conclusion that all those relationships had not worked and had been abusive towards me because I didn´t love myself enough, because in my mind I used to abuse myself with negative and unloving thoughts about myself, because I used to over-eat to hide the emotions I was unable to express, because I didn´t think I was good enough. I was pretty, I was intelligent, but I didn´t love myself enough. I kept attracting men who would mirror my most inner fears right back to me, with abuse or with neglect.

One day I finally knew it was the end. I gathered the courage and I left. I broke his heart, breaking my own heart in the process. I went back to the safe haven of the spiritual realms of Glastonbury, with my dear friend who had been a Mother to me, to heal, to put distance and create a one-way path with no return.

Eventually I returned to Spain, looking for the comfort of Mum´s love and it was there again, in Cádiz, that silver cup in the South of Spain where I grew up, in that sea-side town where this love story was first conceived, where the heartache was so strong that my heart couldn´t take it and it finally broke. And my heart broke into million pieces, making a terrible sound with a painful crack in my chest. He had broken my heart before and every time, with my strong love and my forgiving nature, I would pick up the pieces, glue them together and lovingly mend it, just to bring it back to him again, fully restored, wiser and more loving. But this time, I could see the damage could not be mended. As I looked at my heart, an irreparable pile of dust on the floor, I cried loudly with the fierce intensity of the pain of my broken heart until death found me.

I died… and from my own death I came back, being born anew. I looked up and realized my heart was still beating, I felt it more powerful, radiant and vibrant than ever before. Sadness and heartache had gone, there were no more tears to shed. I then understood that my heart was not broken, I had the wisdom to know now that hearts cannot be broken. PJ came to my life in spiritual service to break the "false" heart concealing my own "true" heart was lying dormant, patiently waiting to be found and let free.

With tears of joy in my eyes I thought of him with so much love, for he had been divinely sent to my service. And in silence, knowing I will never be with him and probably will never see him again, thanked him for setting me free. Free from the need to find outside of myself what was always inside. Free from the false love confused with sexual desire. Free from the continuous search of the man who made me feel the illusion of being complete for a while. Free from the addiction to the idea of romantic love. Free from the separation with my own true essence.

I knew that behind that broken cover, I had found my True Sacred Heart. I had found my True Love: my Essence. I was my True Love. I knew that, from then on, I will be WHOLE as I was nothing else but LOVE. I knew that from that moment, I will live to share with other women how I found my FREEDOM and TRUE LOVE through the path of SELF-LOVE.

ABOUT THE AUTHOR

Gema Ramírez inspires people to raise in consciousness through Coaching, Healing and Mentoring.

She guides people to waking up to greater levels of Joy, to Live from their Heart, to Allow Wellbeing, Happiness and Abundance in their lives, to Love themselves and to Lead Consciously with Peace.

Her passion about her own self-development and spirituality has driven her life. She is a Reiki Master and a Magnified Healing Master Healer. Her professional background is in IT Training, Change Management and Team Leadership.

She is the owner and founder of Sweet Blue Global, where she offers her coaching services and programs. She is the Director of Alienta Coaching UK, bringing to the UK market the ´Coaching and Emotional Intelligent Leadership Program´ that has been changing lives in Spain. She is also the chairman of Shambhala Trust, an educational Trust based in Glastonbury, UK.

CONTACT:

http://www.gemaramirez.com
http://www.sweetblue.global
http://www.alientacoaching.com

PART
TWO

SELF DISCOVERY,
SELF LOVE
AND HOPE

A ROUGH ROAD
Omowunmi Olunloyo: London

*Life was hard for me. People did not know that
I was lonely and sad. That was then. This is
now. Now I am happy, loved and life is great.
"Accept yourself, love yourself, and keep moving
forward. If you want to fly, you have to give up
what weighs you down."*

~ Roy T. Bennett

THE BEGINNING

I was at the darkest point of my life in 2011. It seems like such a long time ago now. I was in a deep pit. I was trying desperately to understand everything that was going on. This season felt like forever, my world was crashing down on me. Each element of my existence was falling apart, piece by piece and it appeared like there was nothing I could do to stop it. I could not change it. I felt so helpless and hopeless.

My life journey was a roller coaster ride, with low and high moments and challenges that I could not control. One of my greatest challenges was accepting that I was enough, that I was good enough just the way I was. Instead of trying to be somebody that I wasn't.

I sacrificed my true purpose for fear of rejection, abandonment, and loneliness. I struggled with low self-esteem and fitting in with the crowd. I could not see past my shortcomings. I felt like a loser. My relationship was affected. I was disrespected, separated, and abused, called all kind of names under the sun and my self-worth was next to nothing.

I attended all kinds of programs and training to prove to myself. I knew I was good enough and should be recognised. I thought I was unattractive and I wanted to change all of that. I did not love myself.

I had wanted to really understand everything that led me to believe that I was not good enough. Did it have to do with the way I was brought up? What had happened in my life to affect me so much now?

NIGERIA

I grew up in a beautiful neighbourhood in Lagos, Nigeria with my two sisters. We were raised by my parents who were very disciplined and principled. Both of my parents are well educated. They were what you would desire in your parents, hardworking, patient, believe the best of you and very loving. My parents, especially my dad is often referred to as "Baba o", which is translated as "my father" by young and old. He was everybody's friend. He was fun, full of life, happy and a very generous giver. My parents expected the best from us, always reminding and encouraging us to go higher.

My childhood left me with many happy memories. When I started secondary school, I was excited. I was just ten years old. I began to encounter different people and situations that challenged who I was. I tried my best to fit in and join the crowd as much as I could.

As I moved from one class year to another, I experienced different issues but it did not seem no matter what I did. I was not good enough. I was not accepted as part of the in-crew. Do not get me wrong, despite all I faced, I had a few friends. They are still friends today and they accepted me as me. At that time, I did not know what they saw in me, but in hindsight I realised there was more to me that meets the eye. In addition, towards the end of my secondary school I was ill. I spent several weeks in and out of hospital recovering, which was a horrible event in my life.

COLLEGE, FAILED RELATIONSHIP AND MARRIAGE

Despite the various challenges in my senior high school, I completed it and secured admission into college. Life became good again. I made new friends and I enjoyed my time at my new college. Everything was going great. I was happy again.

I also started a relationship that was supposed to lead to marriage. After two and a half years it ended abruptly. There was no reason or explanation given. I was devastated as you can imagine. Another rejection that I could not explain.

My self-esteem was knocked back and I began to struggle again. But somehow, I found a way to love again and I entered my second relationship getting married four years later.

For some reason, I thought that because I was now a "MRS", all the issues I had been dealing with would go away. Boy, was I wrong. The shock that I felt as I began to live as a married woman was undeniable. I was dreaming about a fairy tale world where everyone lived happily ever after. My true life was not like this. I struggled to find my place, position, and purpose without my spouse. I could not see how I could do anything without him.

MY JOURNAL

During this period of my life, I found journaling and began to write more frequently. I wrote almost every day about everything that rocked my world, the following extracts are taken from it:

"Do not faint, your time for reward is here so keep at it." This was spoken to me in January 2013 by one of my mentors. I received the word, but did not see how that could happen. I believed in the faith he had in the words he said to me.

"Lord, you know all, and see the heart of everybody, nothing is hid from your sight. I feel out of place, I am not comfortable, I want to serve but I am not being used, it appears as if I am not needed. I am talked on and about, where is the love? I have been told not to

take offense, help me Lord. I need you more than ever. I am lost I need your arms all around me; I want to feel your love right now. Speak to me. If you can use anything Lord you can use me." I wrote this at a time when I was about to give up on everything and I turned to my Lord for help.

In 2014, I wrote, *"Lord, I am not happy right now, I am being told I say things as they are. I feel hurt and disappointed about the feedback. I feel targeted now. I am not pleased. I choose to leave it all to you."*

In 2015, I carried out a purpose quiz online as part of finding myself as I was beginning to love myself. The questionnaire's assessment for me was: Life is good.

You have seen some real breakthrough in your life and you are ready to begin living at the highest levels of the purpose pyramid! It's clear that you have a good understanding of what you what from life and have skills and experience to help you get there. Yet, you might not be fully aware of your purpose, or how to allow it to guide and enhance every aspect of your life. For you, there is still powerful unrealised potential. I was excited at this point because, I was beginning to give myself a break and a chance. I was not being too hard on myself even though I was still battling with not being good enough. The assessment gave me hope.

MY LIGHT BULB MOMENT

After several years of trying to fit in, people pleasing, working hard, really hard, I experienced a light bulb moment. I renewed my mind, I listened to messages that uplifted and gave me hope and gradually over time I was free to be, to do and have effortlessly and that is how my story changed. My favourite book reminded me that as I think in my heart so am I. I started to think happy thoughts so that my actions were powerful, pleasant, and positive. It is what I think that I will become. This is how I transformed my life.

I took responsibility for my action. I began to consciously watch what I allowed to enter my life. I chose to operate by faith. I realised that unless I hear, faith will not come. I was committed to my faith, despite everything trying to stop me believing. Saying and doing is a lifestyle of a believer I was told so since I believed I spoke. I speak to myself a lot, a great deal of my friends can testify to this. My life is a demonstration of the proof that it is possible. I began to see a lot of value in myself. From no hope to having hope; and this hope translates to faith. I received the revelation in the words I heard and it made it easy to speak. It's about believing ladies, that your action dictates your faith.

I cannot say that one particular action transformed me; I believe it was an accumulation of very many small actions that produced the better version of myself that is on display today. I knew that change was coming, I knew I had to show up; I had to come out from the background, from the shadows and shine so brightly and be bold about it. Yes, I felt stuck; but I was ready to live with integrity with my own values, not somebody else's, not my friends, not even society; I acted despite the fear I felt.

STEPS TO CHANGE

Allow me to share with you the steps I took to create my transformation. I decided to love myself, to accept that I was good enough and that I was beautiful. Love is such a powerful force Then I told a few people about my new decision. I saw myself fulfilling the goals of my decision and I used a vision board to bring it to life. I created confessions or affirmation as some like to call it, which I declare daily. As I achieved my goal by taking little action steps, I rewarded myself. This did something to my mind, I believed myself more, and it helped to reaffirm and reinforce my behaviour. For you to have faith, you must hear and believe. I experienced the miraculous when I acted out my faith.

I am more confident, proud, and I love myself so much, you would not believe it. This change in mindset and attitude produced tremendous results in the key core areas of my life. I have launched a weekend retreat program for women where they learn to rest and receive, started a coaching business, published my own magazine and guess who was the cover girl three times in succession? ME. I have published two books and here I am now co-authoring with nineteen amazing women to share a message of hope and possibility. Doors are opening to me because I dared to believe that just maybe I am that special, unique, different, and that is absolutely fine. I am now a minister of enjoyment. I rest and receive.

Perhaps you are going through a similar situation, where you are scared, lonely and afraid but you know deep down inside that there is more to you than what you are currently going through or maybe you have gone through this road before and you are on your way to living fully and showing up, I want to motivate, empower, encourage, educate you. Know this you are valuable, unique, special, different, one of a kind for a reason. Think about it for a moment, please indulge me, do you think you went through all this for nothing? Seriously, the heartache, the sleepless night, the abuse, the loneliness, I do not think so. Are you going to trust your inner voice telling you to step out, to be, to do and to have? Are you going to take your place and manifest your awesomeness? Are you?

In times like this, when my faith is being tried and tested, how I respond defines me. Do I choose to stay afraid, timid, and hidden or do I believe the inner voice that is guiding me and trust it no matter what?

I thought being different was a negative thing but the more I grew up, I realised we are all born to stand out, nobody is born to blend in, you know. How boring would the world be if everyone was the same. I believe each one of us have been put here to touch certain people in their lives and when you do not show up to your life, these people are missing out as well. When you do not do the things, you should be doing you are missing the life you should be living and not communicating the blessings they should be receiving.

ROLE MODELS

My overall message to you is this: Be bold and courageous, to do something different, press on, do not give up or cave in, it is possible and yes you can. If you are alive, there is hope, you are not without hope no matter how it seems. My aim is to encourage and remind you that no matter what you are going through right now, there is light at the end of the tunnel.

And in closing in the words of the First Lady of America Michelle Obama, at her final official emotional farewell speech, so for you reading right now, know that you are enough. Do not ever let anyone or any situation make you feel like you do not matter or that you do not have a place, position, or purpose because you do. And you have a right to be exactly who you are.

I want all women to know that they matter, that they belong, so do not be afraid. do you hear me?

Women, do not be afraid. Be focused be determined. Be hopeful. Be empowered. Empower yourselves with a good education, then get out there and use that knowledge to build an environment, a community, a society worthy of your boundless promise. Lead by example, with hope, never fear. And know that I 'll be with you, rooting for you and working to support you for the rest of my life. And that is true, I know, for every co-author who has contributed their story and their message to this amazing book and who get up every day and work their hearts out to lift up other women.

And am so grateful to all of you for your passion, sense of purpose and your dedication. And I can think of no better way to end my story than celebrating you for taking the bold step to transform your life. So, I want to close by saying thank you. Thank you for believing in yourself enough to invest in your education, your personal development and growth. Being a co-author in the love-unboxed series is one of the greatest honours of my life and I hope I have inspired you and shone a torch of light and hope to you.

ABOUT THE AUTHOR

Omowunmi Olunloyo or Toks as she is known as, is a dynamic speaker and coach who has built her platform of purpose, possibility and power on the years of struggle with low self-esteem, not good enough and trying to fit in. Now a reformed intentional woman on purpose, free from condemnation, lack and self-worth.

Omowunmi is a blogger and writer who helps other women to find their place, position and purpose in life through practical easy step by step actions for good success.

CONTACT:

Facebook: http://www.facebook.com/omowunmi.olunloyo
Twitter: https://twitter.com/OmowumiOlunloyo
Blogger: http://www.omowunmiolunloyo.blogspot.co.uk

DITCHING THE VICTIM IN ME
Dina Marais: South Africa

"People are like stained-glass windows. They sparkle and shine when the sun is out, but when the darkness sets in, their true beauty is revealed only if there is a light from within.

~ Elizabeth Kübler-Ross

EMPOWERING MY VICTIM

I remember the day of my 13th wedding anniversary and how I felt like a victim trapped in a job that I hated, obeying like a good girl, doing what I was told. Well that's what the situation was from my perspective. It took ten years before I was able to objectively understand what was really happening.

I need to take you back to where it started and as in many cases, it began in my childhood. At birth, I briefly died. Fortunately for me, I was brought back to this world by the midwife punching an injection of Lobeline into my heart to stimulate my breathing as I turned from pink to indigo.

Hearing that story from my mother gave me the belief that my soul decided I must be here in this life. For a long time, I wondered why that was so important. My life seemed so insignificant and unworthy for a born-again status.

My childhood must have been a traumatic experience. My mother was ostracized from the church and my father's family because she became pregnant out of wedlock. I feel for her – pregnant at 17 and then to be so brutally rejected and burned at the stake of a perception of righteousness courtesy of an age now passed.

When I was two months old she was pregnant again. Work was scarce. My father, himself only 22, found getting work difficult, so needless to say life was a constant struggle. I can imagine them being without food often and depending on the generosity of others to survive.

As they got older their relationship did not improve. My mother survived the only way she knew how and that was to take control of everything and that included my father.

She was extremely critical of everybody and could only see what was wrong, in her mind. As the eternal victim, she refused to take responsibility for her contribution to any mishap or disaster in her life and blamed others for her misfortune.

My parents fought constantly. There was always something wrong that my mother had to pick on until it became a screaming match, often turning violent with her hurling anything she could get hold of at my father.

Not that he was an angel. Not by a long shot. He could withdraw into his cave and engage in secret financial transactions behind her back. She would only get to know about it when letters of demand arrived in the post box. And true to her nature of taking responsibility for everyone she would make it her problem to pay back the loan. Feeding her victim dragon, she would never let him forget it. She was a master at hauling long-forgotten incidents with no relevance to the current issue to demonstrate that she was the injured party in every case.

My father was absent. I never had the opportunity to forge a deep connection with him as my mother took over everything and there was no space to be without her. I felt abandoned by him not insisting to spend more time with me. I remember an incident when I was about five and I went with my father to his brother's film studio. They were so deeply in discussion that they forgot I accompanied them. The next moment I was alone in this pitch-black place. Lights out and locked up. It probably lasted only a few minutes but it felt like an eternity.

My mother demonstrated her love by being over protective, controlling and critical. Driven by her own fears of failure, losing control and taking everything personally, blaming and labelling were the only ways she knew how to respond. Her strategy was to first see if she was wronged in any way and then launched an attack to defend her position.

No wonder, because as one of ten children and the eldest daughter she had to take care of the younger ones. Her mother was a breeding machine to a man who had a huge appetite for sex and drink and then used her as his punching bag. Many a night the kids fled and hid in the maize fields behind their house as he was on his mission to destroy anything in his path. As a child, I was witness to this violence seeing my grandmother joining my grandfather in his Friday-night drinking spree only to provoke him to hit her head against the wall.

WHO IS GOING TO WIN THIS BATTLE – MY VICTIM OR I?

So I grew up with a lot of baggage. I remember comparing my family to that of my peers and knew there was a huge difference. This started the beliefs that I was not good enough and my family was not good enough. I did not want to be associated with my family because I thought they lacked emotional intelligence, speaking before thinking and in the process, embarrass the hero of their story and themselves. My mother was excellent at telling embarrassing personal details of my father and their relationship issues seemingly totally unaware of how vulgar it sounded and perceived as low-class by the audience.

The more I was judging them, the more I was judging myself. The more I was rejecting them, the more I was actually rejecting myself for not being perfect according to the image I had of who I was supposed to be and the family I was supposed to have. I was ashamed of who I was and where I came from.

Already I tuned into victim-mode. Perceiving myself and my life as being trapped in circumstances beyond my control. I took on my mother's fears of unworthiness, survival and failure.

After school I had a short stint at university and eventually started a career in IT. I enjoyed it then and it was here that I met my husband. He joined the firm and we ended up working closely together. A hunk of a man. I was head over heels the moment I saw him. When he showed interest in me I couldn't fathom what he saw in me and I immediately assumed that he was just planning to use me for a fling.

Although I wanted him so much I was also waiting for the bubble to burst and him to dump me. Fortunately, he persisted and within a year of us meeting each other for the first time we got married.

He told me that when he saw me he felt as if he knew me all along. He knew I was his soul mate and that he was going to marry me. I felt so honoured that he was my man that I just wanted to do everything for him and make sure that he had everything he needed.

Life went on and we had children. I was fortunate to be able to stay at home while they were babies and then moved on to work half-day. When we moved to Cape Town I did not work at all. My husband's career took off and he was promoted to Director hence the move to Cape Town. His new responsibilities of Director meant that he worked long hours, had lunches and dinners multiple times per week and on Saturdays he played golf.

I was lonely and began to feel neglected. I started to resent him for having so much fun in his work meeting new people, doing lunches and dinners and on top of that he played golf on Saturdays while I was stuck with the kids. I wanted to have fun too. I wanted to have alone time, without the kids, with my friends. I decided to confront him about that. I accused him of being selfish and poor me was only good enough to make sure that he and the kids were taken looked after. It was unfair that on top of him never being at home during the week, he was away on Saturdays as well. I said that I also deserved to have fun with my friends. He looked at me and said, "So who is stopping you Dina?"

The question stopped me cold and rendered me speechless. I think my mouth was still open to continue my plea. I realized that I was stopping me. He has never denied me having or doing anything.

To enjoy me-time I made sure that everybody and everything was organized first so that nobody's world was disturbed while I was having fun. However, it rarely played out that way. The moment

I had fun something went wrong with one of the kids and I blamed myself.

Reflecting on this some years later, I realized that I unconsciously omitted to communicate important details with the intention being to sabotage myself. I was constantly beating myself up for not being good enough and blaming myself for causing unnecessary drama in the family.

The kids grew up and went to school. It was time for me to go back to work and we could do with more income. I resisted.

This caused a lot of friction between my husband and me. I had no idea or did not want to know about the financial pressure I put on him. When he asked me about returning to work, I would find every excuse in the book why I couldn't. The kids were old enough to go to day care, but I just could not see myself giving up the privilege of being with them.

When I think back I realized that to continue working in IT no longer interested me. I did not have any other skills or experience; neither did I feel motivated about any type of career. I never had time to discover myself. I had always been controlled by someone, and returning to work meant I would lose this opportunity. This was more important than the money and more important than my husband's happiness.

He arranged a consulting contract for me twice. Both times I just could not focus on my work and the contracts were not extended. He was furious, because he knew these were well within my capabilities. Looking back, I cannot blame him for being frustrated.

He persisted and found a third project and this sounded very interesting. I was in a better place having had some time to reflect.

But soon after I started, our family life started unravelling. I had to leave very early in the morning. This meant that my husband, Johan, was left with crying children to get out in the morning. The youngest was three at the time and just wanted his mother and made it even more difficult for Johan to cope with taking care of the children in my absence.

Typically, I was away from home for 12 hours a day, 5 days a week.

My heart broke when one Friday evening at 7 o'clock my three-year-old called me at the office and said, "Mommy when are you coming home?"

Fast forward a little, it is now our 13th wedding anniversary. Johan is taking me out to dinner. Naturally the conversation went to my work and in my victim-mode I complained about how I disliked IT especially because it took me away from my family. I told him I really wanted to do something else with shorter hours. He retorted, "So who is stopping you, Dina?"

I said, "You!" He replied, "I got that project for you because we needed the money. You are very skilled. Your income makes our lives easier, financially. BUT if there is something else that you want to do, well, let's look at that."

We both agreed that the long hours required by IT projects were not worth the negative impact it had on the children and that I would resign.

I did not know what I wanted to do. All I knew is that I did not want to do IT anymore. I wanted to work with people.

And then the worst thing happened. Johan lost his business and a lot of money as the share market crashed. We now had no jobs, lots of time and no money.

We heard about a business coach. We did not really know about business or life coaches. We decided to attend an event. Something happened. Something was said that opened our minds and helped us discover ourselves and each other. It transformed both our marriage and our careers. We both decided to study Neuro-Linguistic Programming and eventually qualified as NLP Master Practitioners.

I decided to specialize in Neuro-Semantics and PNI – PsychoNeuroImmunology. During my studies, I discovered holes in my own developmental stages as a child. I began to understand the resident fear living in me. In studying quantum physics and neuro-science, I became acutely aware of how we live in the past through our thoughts creating a present reality based on the past.

DISCOVERING THE REAL ME

My life opened up. I could see for the first time how my relationship with myself was the catalyst for the self-sabotage I inflicted upon myself. My relationship with my husband was being damaged by me. I had so many realizations!

For the first time, I realized how distorted my perception was of my relationships. How I filtered everything as being about me. I realized how my fear of not surviving would drive me to even compromise my values to satisfy my needs.

A huge shift for me was that I could give myself permission to accept and love all of me and that my self-worth was unconditional. I could give myself permission to make mistakes and know that my self-esteem was intact. I realized that in my being I am an expression of God and everything else is external and relates to my doing as a human. This separation of my being and doing as a human meant that I did not need to measure my self-worth in terms of what I did or had. What a relief to stop comparing myself to others!

I realized that I did not get upset because of my husband, I got upset because of me. It was my thoughts in my head that upset me. Nobody could make me think, feel, say or do anything. It was all me. This was such a wake-up call. I started to become aware of my own thoughts. It was the end of resentment and blaming. It was also the end of taking criticism and opinions personally.

For the first time, I could understand life from my mother and father's perspective and I realized that they did the best they knew how. My heart filled with compassion and I accepted and appreciated them contributing to my spiritual journey, shaping me into the person I have become and continue to transform into my true self.

VICTIM OR VICTOR

Ultimately, in all our lives there is a choice to be either the victim or the victor.

I could choose to believe that life was happening to me. That I was trapped in a prison of rules and circumstances imposed on me by other people and forces beyond my control. This would result in a life of feeling hopeless-helpless, spiralling depression and blaming everybody and everything except myself for my misery.

Or I could choose to believe that I create my life with every thought, feeling, word and action and that I decide to take response-ability for these creative powers with the intention to purposefully choose the thoughts, feelings, words and actions that would result in me generating feedback that I am living my best life more and more every day.

I chose to be the victor and creator of my life.

NOTE TO THE READER

It doesn't matter where you come from.

It doesn't matter who your family is, your background, you address, your occupation.

It doesn't matter what mistakes you made.

It doesn't matter who you were.

What matters is who you want to be.

Who you know in your heart of hearts is the real you.

Perhaps you still need to get to know her.

You are already perfect and do not need to add anything to make you more perfect.

It's about taking away what disguises the real beautiful you.

Forgive everybody who may have directly or indirectly caused you harm and most of all forgive yourself.

The big decision you need to make now is to commit to connecting and knowing the real you.

This is a continuous journey of self-discovery peeling the onion of your life layer by layer to get to know the core of the amazing real you that you already are.

ABOUT AUTHOR

Dina Marais works is a Relationship Transformation Coach focusing on women who have challenges in their relationships to unleash their personal power and enjoy love life magic.

Whether it is about finding your soul mate, saving your marriage or ending a relationship you have to start with your relationship with your Self and develop your personal power so that you can show up with unshakable inner confidence.

Over more than 14 years of study and practice in NLP – Neuro-Linguistic Programming and Neuro-Semantics, PNI – PsychoNeuroImmunology and Quantum Physics, she has consistently found one simple and powerful truth. She believes that our most important relationship is that with Self because that determines how we experience every facet of our life especially our love life.

CONTACT:

Website: http://dinamarais.com
Email: dina@dinamarais.com
Facebook Page: https://www.facebook.com/dinamaraiscoaching/
Facebook Group: https://www.facebook.com/groups/resetyourdestinypublic/
Twitter: https://twitter.com/DinaMarais
Linked-in: https://za.linkedin.com/in/dinamarais

FALLING IN LOVE WITH ME
Prem Glidden: USA

"I could not, at any age, be content to take my place by the fireside and simply look on. Life was meant to be lived. Curiosity must be kept alive. One must never, for whatever reason, turn her back on life."

– Eleanor Roosevelt

IN THE BEGINNING

My journey begins in a little Orthodox Jewish neighbourhood in Baltimore, Maryland. I was born in the early 1950's, to parents who were the first generation in our family to be born in the United States. My grandmother (my father's mother) lived with us and my aunts and uncles and cousins lived close by. Out of 8 grandchildren, I was the only girl, so, there was a lot of excitement around my arrival. And, they had a very clear idea of who I needed to be to fulfil my role in the family and be the daughter they wanted me to be.

From an early age, I loved everyone. It didn't matter to me what colour you were or what religion you practiced, I talked to everyone. And this was incredibly upsetting to my family as they came from a world where much of their family had been killed in the Holocaust and they, themselves, had experienced great prejudice as Jews living in the US. They believed, that the only way to be safe, was to stay within the confines of our own people and community which, honestly, made no sense to me. So, I kept asking questions which made my parents incredibly angry as questions were not acceptable in our family system. One was to learn the rules and follow them. All I knew was that I was a huge disappointment to my Mom and Dad and this made me very sad. The only one who seemed to understand me and love me for myself was my Bubby (grandmother in Yiddish). Bubby was my roommate, our bedroom was a little room off the kitchen with two twin beds, side by side. I adored her. She was my best friend and my protector, always standing up for me, when my parents would get angry at me for not obeying their directives.

When I was 9, Bubby had a heart attack and died suddenly. My grief seemed to have no ending as the one person I could count on to protect me and be there for me was gone.

FORBIDDEN LOVE

Eventually I adapted, I did my best to avoid angering my parents and just tried to be as invisible as possible. That strategy seemed to work okay until the summer of 1967, when I was 15 years old. That was the summer I met a lovely Catholic boy, with big blue eyes and a sweet caring heart. We fell in love almost instantly and as I suspected would happen, I was forbidden to see him.

I didn't understand why and when I tried to talk to my father, he told me that I was too young to understand but that one day, he would turn on me and call me a "Damn Jew." All I could do was shake my head incredulously as I knew there was no way that could ever happen. My father looked at me with sad and disappointed eyes. Why couldn't I just be a good girl and trust that they knew what was best for me?

We tried to break up – over and over again. But somehow, we would see each other and the attraction and power of first love was just too strong. So, I would lie and sneak and get caught. They would punish me and scream at me, listen to my phone calls and forbid me from leaving the house. Most of the time I just felt hopeless and very sad as I truly never wanted to hurt or upset anyone.

College could not have come sooner for me. Suddenly, I was meeting people from all over the world, hearing about subjects and topics that were completely new to me and I felt an insatiable desire to learn and study and grow. I became a seeker, seeking to understand myself and the universe in a deeper and more profound way. During my Sophomore year, a boy that I had grown close to was killed in a car accident. That experience turned out to be a major turning point in my life. Unable to process my feelings and grief, I gained 75 pounds over the next 6 months. I also became clear that what I needed to learn, was not going to be found in a University system. A few months later, I dropped out of school and my friend and I headed south in her VW bug.

MY SPIRITUAL JOURNEY BEGINS

We drove and camped, meeting many fellow seekers along the way. On my travels, I had the opportunity to take a kundalini yoga class at a centre in Houston and I loved it. Eventually I knew it was time to head back to Baltimore and rather than live with my parents, I got an apartment with one of my high school friends. I found out that there was a kundalini yoga ashram about 20 minutes away and I started to go to classes. At first, I could barely sit cross legged on the floor. I was over 200 pounds and very out of shape. But there was something safe and warm about the yoga centre. I loved being there. Even though I didn't have a clue where I was headed, I knew that this was the vehicle to take me where I needed to go. The first time I met Yogiji, the spiritual leader of this community of ashrams, he gave me the spiritual name, "Prem", which means love. He told me that this was to be my journey in this lifetime, to understand love. I had no idea at the time how true these words would become and the person I needed to learn to love the most was myself.

Every ounce of me knew that this was my path, so I jumped in with both feet. I loved every part of it, getting up early to meditate, doing yoga and chanting moved me in a way that I had never felt before. Even wearing the traditional "uniform" of the ashram – all white kurta, churidars and a turban to cover the hair, worked for me as I felt it gave me an identity that felt good to me.

One area I was still struggling with was my food addiction and the teacher in the ashram in Baltimore suggested I might be best served to spend the summer in the Tucson ashram where they specialized in addictive behaviour.

Again, my life was about to change in miraculous ways. I flew to Tucson, where the ashram was a 28-bedroom ex-Fraternity house on the University of Arizona campus. I arrived early one morning and was asked to come into the room of the Ashram Director. I walked in and sat down on the floor on a mat in front of the most beautiful blue eyes I had ever seen. He smiled at me and said "You have no idea how beautiful you are, do you? Well, you and I are going to work together and in the end, you will know that you are an incredible woman and any man would be blessed to have you in his life." I just sat there with tears rolling down my face. I had never felt so seen and so loved in my entire life.

BECOMING PREM

An important part of my journey of transformation began on that fateful morning. Over the next few months, I fasted, I moved my body, I did a lot of yoga and over time I lost the extra 75 pounds that I had gained. I moved permanently to Tucson, and became the Secretary of the ashram and assistant to the Director. I began to see myself as a leader and someone who had value.

Part of the culture of the ashram, was that Yogiji, our spiritual teacher arranged your marriage. With my history, I was okay with that, it made me feel safer that I didn't need to trust that someone would fall in love with me and want to be with me. My first marriage lasted just a few years and produced a beautiful son. Once that divorce was final, when my son was only two, Yogiji decided that I should marry the man who was head of the ashram in Fairbanks, AK. So off we went from the warmth of Tucson, to the frigid north of Alaska. Another huge opportunity to grow!

Suddenly, I was the co-leader of an Ashram where 9 people lived. This turned out to be a mixed experience for me. In my outer world, I could apply the leadership skills I learned in Tucson and I began to teach yoga and meditation in the community and at the University and loved it. And they loved me. But inside, I still had a lot of anger that I had not even begun to process. I was clingy and insecure and often angry in my relationship with my husband and took it as a personal rejection if he wanted to do anything without me. Which, of course, just pushed him away more and created evidence for me that I continued to be a big disappointment to those that loved me and undeserving of being loved. And I felt deeply ashamed about being angry and insecure as those were certainly not the qualities of a "spiritual" woman.

We lived in Alaska for 8 years, and in 1989 when a business opportunity came up in the Midwest we made a move from the woods of Alaska to the middle of Chicago. Once we settled in there, my awareness of my inner unhappiness continued to grow and one day I picked up a local newspaper and called an ad to make an appointment with a therapist in my neighbourhood. He had a loving and kind presence and I began to work with him in both group and individual therapy. He began to help me unravel my deep patterns of invisibility and during our time of working together, I made my transition out of the ashram lifestyle back into the "normal" world. It had become clear to me that it was time for me to learn to not look outside myself for wisdom but that I needed to form an inner relationship with my own inner guidance and higher self. This was a big step for me as I had been "hiding" behind my spiritual garb for almost 20 years and I was deeply afraid that no one would know who I was without it.

FALLING IN LOVE WITH ME

I finally began to feel a sense of safety and connection with myself in a way that I had never experienced before. Now I just had to learn to translate that into my relationship with others. And the truth is, I didn't have a clue what it looked like to be my authentic self with others in a way that felt safe to me. I still woke up every day in my marriage feeling rejected. I was still a major people pleaser, not even sure about what I wanted or needed because no one had ever bothered to ask me.

The crazy thing is, most people would not have had a clue that I felt this way. My husband and I started a business together and once again, I rose to the top in leadership in our company, our industry and our community. I was a great sales person, passionate about what I believed in and able to share it in a way that inspired others. But in my intimate relationships, I was a failure – unhappy and angry, feeling unseen and unloved.

Eventually my husband and I divorced and I moved into a lovely little condo in downtown Chicago. I had two relationships after my divorce that ended painfully and disappointingly. Even though I was successful in many places in my life, I felt so frustrated and confused as to why I could not seem to create healthy, happy, sustainable love in my life. Through my therapy and personal growth work I had done so far, I certainly had grown a lot in my self-esteem and understood the impact that my childhood experiences had for me. I just wasn't sure how to translate that into the love and partnership that I so deeply desired. I honestly don't think I really believed it was possible to be loved in the way that I wanted but I was willing to not be the reason why. Which for me, meant, I was willing to bare my soul open and authentically and honestly look at all the beliefs that I held about myself, others and life that created aloneness and separation.

In that place of deep possibility and ferocity, life showed up to support me. A friend gave me several CD's by Abraham-Hicks and it was life-changing for me, filling in so much in my understanding of how I was the creator of my own life experience. I was given a book called "Calling in "The One, by Katherine Woodward Thomas that spoke to me about "falling in love" with me and becoming the Beloved that I so deeply desired. I was so moved, I called Katherine and ask to work one on one with her to uncover the deep beliefs and ways of being that were keeping me stuck in the patterns of the past. Little by little, I began to understand, the beliefs and strategies of that little girl who did not know how to survive any other way. I learned that I needed to honour her as up until now, I hated her. She was whiny and needy and I was angry that she could not seem to get it together. Then I realized, that I was treating her the way she had been treated her whole life – like she was inappropriate and needed to be someone different for me to love her.

I learned that I needed to figure out what it was that I wanted and needed and that my needs mattered. I was so busy always organizing around others so they would be happy with me that it never occurred to me to think about what I needed. Then once I knew what I needed, I just had to learn the skills to ask for it. Another major muscle that I needed to grow. I realized that in a world where I was a disappointment and unworthy of love that I had learned ways of being that concurred with that conclusion and continued to bring me evidence of its validity. To shift that, I needed to build a foundation based on a deeper truth, that I was perfect just the way that I am and deeply deserving of loving and being loved. From there, I could be curious - what if I decided to source my happiness and value from within myself? What would it look like to be a woman in the world who knows her value? Who would I be being? How would I show up?

FINDING THE LOVE OF MY LIFE AT AGE 62

So, this has been my journey and in the end I now understand that it has been a journey of falling in love with me. And along the way, two years ago, at 62 I met the love of my life. He is everything I have ever written on any list anywhere. And we are having so much fun sharing life together. We live in the same community as my parents and I now have a loving and close relationship with them that I never thought possible. Because my life has been filled with so many miracles, I work with women all over the world standing with them in releasing their beliefs and patterns of the past and supporting them to align with the present and future that they are so deserving of. Every day I am grateful that I had the courage to be a stand for the deeper truth of who I am and what was possible for me.

ABOUT THE AUTHOR

Prem Glidden is an International Transformative Coach and Healer deeply committed to "being the change she wants to see in the world." She is a powerful guide in supporting those she works with to achieve their greatest possibilities in life and in love.

Prem is a Certified Coach in several modalities including; Calling in "the One," and Conscious Uncoupling, personally trained by founder, Katherine Woodward Thomas. She is an Intuitive Healer, certified in the Lifeline Technique, developed by Dr Darren Weissman. She is a Minister of Peace with the Beloved Community and has been a teacher of Yoga, Meditation and Pranayama for over 40 years.

Prem lives in Florida with her beloved partner, Bob and her kitty, Bailey; sharing a lovely condominium overlooking a lake. Her life is a wonderful example of what is possible and that it is never too late to change your life in miraculous ways!

CONTACT

http://www.premglidden.com

FROM LOST SOUL TO LIVING A LIFE LESS CAGED
Michelle Catanach: United Kingdom

We're born alone, we live alone, we die alone. Only through our love and friendship can we create the illusion for the moment that we're not alone.

~ Orson Welles

IT IS NOT ALWAYS POSSIBLE TO LOOK ON THE BRIGHT SIDE

Have you ever wanted to die? I am not talking about wishing the ground under your feet would open up and swallow you in one of those excruciatingly embarrassing moments. I mean real death. The one in which you will be pushing up daisies kind of death for a long time afterwards. The kind when you truly, genuinely do not want to live anymore. The kind when you deliberately plan, with all intent and purpose, to attempt suicide.

This is not the cry for help or to seek attention type with the hope a prince in shining armour will ride up on a white horse and save you kind.

It is because you have a complete and undeniable belief that the world would be a happier and better place without you contributing another second of your worthless existence.

That is how I felt in 2001. I was nineteen years old.

I remember that night as if it were yesterday. I enjoying a drink with friends in our regular haunt. It was that period in my life when I spent every night out boozing for fear of missing out. Alcohol filled the void of what was an otherwise unexciting life. I did not even have any hobbies. I would wake up, go to work then to the pub. A pattern repeated each day and every single day. Wash, rinse, repeat.

That night I drank more than usual and became drunk. Booze made me a more fun and exciting person to be around, helping me lose my inhibitions and create a mask of confidence. It helped me to take my mind off the emptiness I felt inside.

I was grieving that night, or at least that's how it felt. The loss of my ex after yet another volatile breakup had left me in a state of mourning.

I remember drinking copious amounts of vodka to hide my sadness. I was free of him, so should have been celebrating, not drowning my sorrows. He was a complete bastard. Everyone told me so. Yet I didn't see it. More than two years of torment and manipulation meant I was co-dependent and needy, convinced that I was nothing without him, believing that I needed him to survive. I was laughing on the outside, flirting with anyone with a pulse, yet crying on the inside, the voices and insecurities getting stronger the more inebriated I became.

The walk home was long and lonely without him by my side, yet the torment and abuse would have been unbearable if he was. I trudged through puddles, the rain drowning me and leaving me looking scruffy and bedraggled. I looked old for my nineteen years. The way I walked, the clothes I wore and the pained expression set in my face, far removed from the vibrant and happy girl I had once been.

I found myself calling him, begging him to take me back, sobbing as he screamed a torrent of abuse and profanities down the phone.

He was right. I was a slag. A nutcase. A whore.

No one wanted me. Why would they? Even my family were ashamed and embarrassed by me.

At least he had wanted me. He had pitied me and taken the burden off someone else by being with me. He had done the world a favour; taken one for the team as they say, now even he had walked away. He could not bear the burden any longer.

At least that is what he made me believe.

I felt so alone. I did not have anyone to talk to. I had spent so many years believing that showing emotion and asking for help was a weakness. I did not know how to express about my feelings. If anyone took the time to ask, I would smile like a good girl, saying everything was ok. I kept all my pain, sadness and loneliness bottled up inside.

The truth was I was addicted to him like a crack addict needing that next fix. I needed him. Without him I felt I was nothing. He gave me a reason to wake up every morning even if it meant crying myself to sleep at bedtime.

A DARK DECISION

I remember reaching home. Still swaying as I fumbled around for my door key, tear-stained and bleary eyed. I staggered down the hallway and into the kitchen. The gaudy green and orange cupboards illuminated in the moonlight.

At this point I was not really thinking anything. I knew what I had to do. It had been an easy decision to make. I did not even consider the outcome. The effect it would have on the people around me. What would it matter; I would be dead.

The house was eerily silent as I opened the kitchen cupboard where I knew a stash of pills were stored. My hand blindly grappled around in the dark, rattling condiments and tins as I reached to the back of the cupboard. I pulled out whatever I could find.

I took as many as a could; one by one. Rapidly pushing my feelings of self-loathing, loss and loneliness down with every swallow. Praying, praying that whatever they were, they would work to end my existence. I wanted to vanish from this world.

I have no memory of how many I took. I did not even know what I was taking. I did not care. They were drugs. Pills. They had to kill me if taken in excess. Right?

In my selfishness, I did not give a "shit" about the outcome. No-one gave a "shit" about me, so why should I give a "shit" about them? I simply focused on the task in hand. I was so angry with me, the world, the universe.

And then I went to bed.

THE AFTERMATH

I awoke dazed and confused, my head throbbing as the room spun. I vomited into a pint glass that was on the floor beside my bed. Initially, impressed with myself that I had avoided spewing on the carpet.

Then it hit me, like a juggernaut at 100mph.

I was still alive.

To this day, I will never forget the wave of disappoint engulf my entire body as I realised that my attempt to end it all had failed. All the feelings of hurt, pain, hatred and despair came flooding in like a tsunami, leaving me in a crumpled, sobbing heap on my bed. I was so useless; I could not even take my own life properly. I felt like I was grieving all over again.

Of course, I carried on like nothing had happened, leaving the house that morning, my mum ranting as I left, affirming everything I already knew about me being a useless waste of space.

Me being late for work with what she believed was simply yet another hangover only added more fuel to her flame.

I called in sick at work then spent two hours sitting on the swing of a children's playground, head in hands, routinely vomiting as my body desperately tried to expel the toxins.

No one knew what I had done.

In fact, it took several years before I confessed to anybody, and before writing this only three people knew what happened in my despair.

I would like to say that this experience woke me up. That I saw that I had a second chance in life. Something to live for. That I would radically transform and live out my soul's desires. I would find my passion in life and spend my time trying to attain it.

But it did not. It was simply another chapter of a deeply troubled life that in all truthfulness had not reached rock-bottom from its spiral downwards from the age of sixteen.

WHO ARE YOU TO JUDGE?

Please do not judge me. I know what you as my readers must be thinking about me. Is she so selfish and self-centred that she has no respect for the people around her? Why can she not see she has been gifted a second chance to find her way again. Well, not all stories have silver linings.

I needed my fix, my drug, my cocaine, my high, my pain, my self-loathing, so I got back with my ex again that night. We even moved in together. So, began six months of emotional bullying, the odd black-eye and bruised ribs. I went to work struggling to make ends meet while he bummed around smoking pot all day.

Such was his power, his control, that everyone thought it was me. I was the problem. They saw a crazed, nagging girlfriend. Yet what they didn't see was the powerless girl reacting to whispered threats and muttered taunts while he acted like the innocent, downtrodden charming boyfriend to the outside world.

I absolutely despised the guy, but felt too weak to leave. I fell into a deeper depression, stuck in a limbo of not wanting to be at home and not wanting to be at work. Not wanting to be anywhere. Until one day I found myself with my hands around his throat, squeezing it tight, desperately trying to rid myself of this nightmare that I had found myself living in.

For a moment, I really wanted to kill him. To end the torture.

The only thing that stopped me was the thought of a prison sentence. And he really was not worth it.

It was then that I knew I had to leave.

HAD I SEEN THE LIGHT?

This triggered several years of self-destructive behaviour as I found solace in anything that would make me feel validated, loved or simply numb the pain.

Drugs, excessive drinking, countless one-night-stands, toxic friendships, excessive dieting, binge eating, rebounding from one job to another, clinging on to lousy men while pushing away any chance of happiness. Anything that made me feel good while supporting a deeply embedded unconscious belief that I was not worthy enough.

I was a far cry from the straight A student of my school days who had showed so much promise and potential. And a far greater cry from the baby given the spiritual name of joy for the delight she would supposedly bring to other people's lives.

THE RETURN OF JOY

I had become comfortably numb as the song goes. I was nobody. I felt nothing, had no identity, no life just existence. It seemed I had been lost for a lifetime.

Then one day, I had my "Forest Gump" moment. No!! I did not start running as real running. I had been running away all my life. This time I was going to run with purpose. I made the decision to travel.

Travelling had been a dream of mine for years, but I had been so sucked in to by my boozy lifestyle and toxic relationships that I did not have the motivation – or self-belief - to actually do it; only lame excuses to distract me.

When you feel positive, well that is when positive things get attracted to you. I met Steve. He had already travelled the world on two occasions. He took me on holiday to Cambodia and after being so touched by the experience, it was then that I knew: I had to travel.

I asked Steve to join me. Reluctantly he agreed. Our first year together had been hell (for him). So, convinced was I that he was just like all the others that I constantly tried to provoke him to prove my belief that all men were arseholes. In reality I was the aggressor, often violently lashing out after too much drink. He, of course, never retaliated.

Travelling was the making of me and while it forces many couples apart, it brought Steve and I closer together. Away from the people, places and situations that triggered my insecurities, I was able to see things clearly.

I finally understood love, compassion and humanity. I understood how the world really worked, witnessing genuine innate happiness in people with materially poor lives. I observed pure joy and gratitude despite obvious hardship and often traumatic pasts.

I realised that Steve was not like all the others and that he was in fact a decent bloke (and double brownie points for putting up with so much of my shit when most men would simply walk away)

But most of all, I made peace with myself. I accepted myself and no longer felt ashamed of who I was.

When I stood on top of a relatively small mountain in Australia's Warrumbungle National Park on my 26th birthday, for the first time in 10 years I felt free. I had finally left the bullshit of the past behind.

Joy had found her way home

SPIRALLING INTO THE SHADOW

Following that day, life became pretty phenomenal. I overcame eating issues and shed a load of weight (without even trying). I drastically cut down on the booze. I discovered hobbies and a passion for learning. I cycled from London to Paris and ran my first half marathon, feats that before I would not have considered trying. I had more travelling adventures. I attracted some amazing people into my life, forming deep and meaningful connections and my career, which had always been a non-starter, soared.

And remember Steve? Against all odds, we got married (in Vegas!) and now have two gorgeous children (and this despite my own resistance and belief that I did not deserve kids)

Then I followed my dream. I left work to have baby number 2, set up a business then BOOM!

I DID WARN YOU ABOUT SILVER LININGS!

All of the crap about me not being good enough, stuff that I thought I had overcome. Well the truth is I had just filed it away. I had not addressed the other me. The real me? I was locked away in the shadowy depths of my mind waiting to be found. I was found and I came back with vengeance.

I felt my life spiralling downwards again. All those old feelings of shame and self-loathing were creeping back. I felt like a failure. I was a terrible mother. An even more terrible wife. My business was a sinking ship weighted down by mounting debt.

I started drinking more alcohol than normal, bingeing on junk and not taking very good care of myself.

I retreated into myself, pushing people away and felt ashamed for imagining life without my kids. The stress and overwhelm was all consuming and I simply did not recognise the person I was anymore. I only knew I did not like who I was becoming.

TURNING MY WOUNDS INTO MY WORK

Then it happened. My 3-year-old daughter hit me. Really hit me! My anger took over. In that moment, all my pent up frustration came out as I picked her up by her shoulders and shouted loudly in her face, took her to her room and threw her - like a rag doll - onto her bed.

When I saw her sobbing inconsolably, pleading with me with her eyes, it's like I woke up.

I saw me. My inner child who wanted nothing more than to be loved. And I realised in that moment that I had turned into my mum and all the women before her, unleashing generations of wounds, patriarchal patterns and insecurities onto the one person I had always vowed to protect.

I knew that I wanted better for my daughter. I knew that I wanted her to grow up free from insecurity and pain, to be able to fully express herself, to love herself, to be loved and know her worth and give her the freedom to live HER life, not mine.

When I looked at my daughter, full of unconditional love, so pure and innocent, when I realised that her challenging. behaviour was a mirror, of me. I knew that I had to set myself free from my shadow.

The generations of hurt and wounding had to stop with me so that I could leave a better legacy for my children.

NOTE TO THE READER

Who you are being – not what you are doing – has the greatest impact on your children.

If you want to raise children who are deeply connected to who they really are and live as the fullest expression of themselves – physically, emotionally and spiritually including all the messy parts - then YOU need to be the change. YOU need to be that person.

You need to stand in your own power, walk your own path and live as the most authentic embodiment of you because it gives your children permission to do the same.

Truth will set you free and will not only heal you, but past and future generations too.

ABOUT THE AUTHOR

Michelle Catanach - Speaker, Kids Mentor, Intuitive Coach and founder of www.theuncagedrevolution. com – helps sensitive & soulful mamas uncage themselves, their kids and their lives using the power of consciousness, connection and creativity. She helps mums connect with their divine wisdom, heal generational wounds, bust through old paradigms and set their souls free so that they can authentically lead the next generation. Her mission is to transform the way we collectively raise and educate our kids, from a fear-based to soul-centred approach. Michelle believes that when you empower a mum you empower a child and THAT is how we change the world.

RESOURCE

www.theuncagedrevolution.com/unparent to access her free audio series 'How to Unparent Yourself'

A MELODY OF SORTS
Joh Johnson: London

"Some people feel the rain, others just get wet"
Bob Marley

CHILDREN KNOW

I see patterns, the hidden links, and sometimes even the bigger picture. The strings that tie us together, the thread you don't know is there. The energy that flows with the tides of change and the colours that invites a mood. The shapes that define our thoughts and the wind that whispers in our ear ever so slightly when we remember our breath. I feel the vibrations that touch us ever so tenderly when our souls sometimes cry from the feelings that make us want to hide.

As a child, I often felt disconnected in school. One teacher in particular would get very annoyed repeatedly saying, "Stop dreaming Joanne come back into the room." I'd get swallowed up in my own imaginations where school seemed like a nonsensical mystery. I'd yawn endlessly with absolute boredom waiting for the day to end so that I could dream uninterrupted and enter a world that seemed more real.

The journey to and from school left me captivated in the summer months as I basked in the sunlight of intoxicating smells with the blooming flowers and its light fantastic spectrum of colours I could almost taste. Not even the wasps and the bees that readily kissed this dizzying display could deter me as I sought not to understand these intriguing patterns, shapes, and perfect symmetrical blooms, but simply to absorb an energy that felt like freedom. I'd stand long enough to breathe its scent, feel its energy, then I'd hear, "Stop dreaming Joanne."

TO CREATE IS TO LIVE

I recognised my creativity and followed a path that expressed this perfectly. By the age of twenty-one, I had trained as a Fashion Designer and literally cloaked myself in more colours, textures and feelings that fed an energy which captured the spirit of the time.

We were both nineteen when I met this man who I was to spend more than a decade with. He was at music college studying classical music and I was at fashion college. We fed each other's creative spirits with a rare freedom hard to find. He formed a band in the early 80's where his musical genius, considered by many, to have helped shape the face of Black British music.

Meanwhile, I supplied a couple of shops on the Kings Road, had my own stall in Covent Garden in front of the Piazza, and designed for some artists in the music industry, including him. With much of the early material written in our home at the time, music featured big in my life as I absorbed this force locking into an energy that synchronised beautifully with my own as I stayed in the preferred background.

DEAR FORK, WHICH ROAD PLEASE?

They say that when things come too quickly they can disappear just as fast; and they did. We were young and by the age of twenty-five we'd had a daughter. We'd gained much in a few years and then lost virtually everything by the time we were thirty. Separation followed with much sadness in tow and the road ahead was to be a long drive home.

Luckily, I had a good family support network and it was time for me to start over. I was in survival mode and had a child to take care of. Permanently stressed, I regained much in a short space of time, and within five years I'd got a degree and bought myself another home in 2001.

DO I LIVE OR DIE TRYING

Stress they say is a necessary evil unless it kills you. I remember that I never really made a consistent and conscious effort to check my breasts. It was my then boyfriend who found a lump in my left breast. I was convinced it was nothing more than a cyst. I reluctantly went to the doctors and he referred me to the hospital, just in case. Seen within two weeks, I was sent for a mammogram, a biopsy followed, which eventually proved conclusively that a cyst had been wishful thinking. In May 2005 I was diagnosed with breast cancer on the same day as Kylie Minogue.

Standing in the shower that night, I cried for the world for what seemed like hours, and like a baby, stopped eventually through sheer exhaustion. I went to bed wondering if I would live or die.

MORE THAN MY BODY

Mum called the next day and her words were a blur. I felt fine, looked fine and was not in any pain. I wondered if I was dreaming. Wanting to gain a semblance of normality I started to clean the house. With hoover in hand I stopped dead in my tracks as I heard a voice say,

"You are not your body."

Suddenly a calmness came over me that I cannot describe and spent the remainder of the day in silent contemplation.

I hated hospitals with a preference for natural health, I wondered how on earth I would get through this. The internet was awash with information on natural cures for cancer. I didn't know what to believe and quickly became overwhelmed. I needed to stop, rest and be taken care of so I dutifully followed the doctors rushed orders.

KILLING ME

Surgery followed with six rounds of planned chemotherapy. My hair began falling out by the second round and I felt like shit! Looking ridiculous I simply shaved my head. Oddly I felt exhilarated, liberated even.

During treatment, the next day was always the worst. Feeling like a bout of extreme food poisoning, and have a truck drive over you, reverse backwards several times — that's pretty much my experience of chemo in a nutshell. I couldn't get out of bed for days and would crawl to the toilet on my hands and knees vomiting as I went. The chemo seemed to kill me every time and I thought one day, like bloodletting, this would be considered barbaric. Some women did ok, I didn't.

The anti-sickness pills didn't help and I lost all interest in food. I couldn't taste anything anyway. I started to get double vision and all my nails turned black. My weight plummeted quickly and I looked like a cancer victim.

I'd coloured my greying hair for years, but after this I vowed 'no more'. I quickly grew to understand the toxicity of putting such chemicals on your hair that then effortlessly seep into your bloodstream to poison your whole body, including breast tissue.

Breast cancer affects everything supposedly associated with what it is to be and feel like a woman — your breasts, your hair and your womb. I was lucky I had my daughter and didn't lose my breast and I knew my hair would grow back.

After the fifth round of chemo I chose to abandon all further conventional treatment. I could feel my spirit imploding on itself — no more chemo, no radiation and no drugs. My family knew how head strong I am and I had made my choice. I cleaned up my diet and most importantly explored my emotions. Like so many, I wanted to fix the world and stuff my emotions back down my throat. I felt it was no coincidence that the cancer was in my left breast directly above my heart. Disappointment after disappointment had left me 'broken' hearted.

CANCER BLOODY CANCER

The following year I went back to work but by July 2006 Dad was diagnosed with bowel cancer. By the end of the year Dad was dying, and so was Mum. Several days before Christmas Mum was diagnosed with the deadliest of cancers; pancreatic cancer. It was considered terminal too. That's three members of the same family diagnosed with cancer within two years. I was to be the only survivor and had been on both sides now. For me it was harder watching somebody die than being that person who could die.

During this time, I developed panic attacks where I couldn't breathe. I couldn't get enough air in and I had to remember to take deep breaths so as not to pass out. I struggled knowing that the stress could bring back the cancer and so I had to be fearless with death and hoped for the best.

It was a heart-breaking time for my family but we grew strong. My Dad had been full of regrets for a life less lived before he died. With Mum, I could speak openly of death and its transcendence. She followed some of my advice and lived for twelve months instead of the estimated three.

Then came the time to pull back as I sensed my ancestors letting me know they would take over now. In January 2008, weary and tired Mum was gone from this physical world, I sensed her spirit become vibrant — free of a body that no longer served her. To me she began to live again, just like I felt my Dad did the year before. I felt her dancing in a world I couldn't see.

DO NOT FOLLOW, LEAD

In the years that followed I've learned to speak my truth, follow my spirit, trust my path and honour the soul that I am. Women recently diagnosed, known and unknown would call me. We'd just talk and I'd share my experience hoping it would ease their pain in some way. I'd say do what your spirit tells you not what I do or did. You want to help others, do it from a position of strength and put yourself first so that you are strong. In my experience women with breast cancer had a common thread of wanting to help others and putting themselves last. Some died, some lived, and I was as much a part of their journey as they were mine.

Already qualified in Reiki and Massage, I trained further in emotion based therapies including Theta Healing, Hypnotherapy, NLP and Emotional Freedom Technique, and I knew it was my thinking that kept me strong. The most profound healing tool was yet to come.

REALITY IS WRONG, DREAMS ARE REAL

It was Boxing night December 2011 and I headed off to bed where I'd pretty much nodded off straight away. At some point during the night it felt like I'd been woken up from my sleep, except I knew I wasn't awake. Lying on my back, I was aware that I was also the observer of myself sleeping.

Looking through closed eyes I started to see the most mystical of images against the wall to my right. I watched in amazement as cartoon characters from my long-forgotten childhood came alive. Characters like Daffy Duck, Speedy Gonzales and Bugs Bunny, intertwining into one big show with the added sound effects. I could see flickering lights like fairy dust weaving in and out into one big magical display. At times, it felt like a wonderland of thoughts created in my head then projected out onto the wall in real time. I felt wide awake, yet I knew I was fast asleep.

Suddenly I thought, "I wonder if mum is here?" I looked to my left and there she was, sitting at the end of my bed looking peaceful and happy, arms gently folded on her lap with a smile that exuded a secret I might one day know.

Mum had died almost three years previous and I could only wonder what had happened in that time. In my excitement, I began asking her so many questions, almost not waiting for an answer, "Where are you? How have you been? What are you doing? Are you ok?" She'd respond with, "Well you know," shrugging her shoulders, with more, "Well you know?" Her coyness told me that maybe I'm not supposed to know.

Ducking and diving she reached forward with one hand as if to distract me from all the questions. Getting closer I could see every vessel filled vein with blood running through it as if showing me she was very much alive. Suddenly I could hear footsteps coming closer. Was I beginning to wake up? The door to my right opened, and it was my brother, "Did you see Mum" I asked. I looked to my left and Mum had gone, but there snuggled up in the crux of my elbow was a teddy bear. At that point I woke up, no brother in sight I knew I'd been sleeping and I just knew I'd met Mum again.

WHEN OUR ANCESTORS SPEAK, LISTEN WELL

Mum came back the following night with the simple words, "You'll love this." I was taken by the hand, whisked away as if speeding through time and space then suddenly coming to an abrupt halt. We were in what felt like an ancient healing space and in the middle, was a large stone slab, like an operating table with a live body on it. With sand stone walls stretching up as far as the eye could see, it opened to a skylight. With the sunlight streaming through, it bought much needed natural light.

In front of the body was a man holding what looked like a guitar. He appeared to be moving up along the body starting at the feet. He'd listen to the body, then adjust the guitar strings, play the guitar against the body, then listen again. Repeating this all the while moving up towards the head. Confused I knew that something both medical and musical was going on, a form of healing I'd never before come across.

As soon as I 'understood', Mum whisked me away again to an even bigger cave like area. I could see a big Gong as used in rank films that you'd bang in the middle at the start or ending of a movie. Except he played around the outer rim, not in the centre. I was given just enough information again to go away and make sense of. Suddenly I woke up and Mum was gone and it was early morning. What a journey! My body felt rested but I remembered every detail.

LIVE THE DREAM

That morning I wasted no time searching the internet for clues that would give meaning to my dream. I looked for healing with guitars, guitars on the body, strings on the body — then I came across 'Tuning Forks'. Put simply, I found that Tuning Forks sort of 'tune' and bring balance to the body. That's got to be it? Seconds later, I found the Gong I'd seen in the dream too. And yes, it could indeed be played around the rim. Could this be another healing tool?

The information that followed blew my mind as I began to connect so many dots; the colours, energy, music, art, movement, shapes, sacred geometry, science, medicine, vibration, and feelings. I was reliving my childhood all over again. Within 48 hours I was studying Sound Healing on an online course.

I'd tapped into an Ancient Healing Spiritual system that encapsulated the energy of sound as a creative force used in rites of passage, sacred ceremonies, shamanism, healers, priests, priestesses, and medicine men from all corners of the earth.

THE POWER OF SOUND

As Sound Healers, we use our voice, mantra, colours, the chakras, musical notes, the planets, silence, the breath, and healing instruments that go back thousands of years. Tuning forks are to be found in the Ancient hieroglyphs in Egypt. The Gong goes back 6000 years to Ancient Sumeria (Iraq) and the beginning of the bronze age. You experience stillness, peace and clarity, the easing of physical, mental and emotional pain, and so much more.

Sound is all around us and there is no getting away from it. Every sound has a frequency and carries a vibration that can have a positive or negative effect on our mind, body and spirit. The ear is the organ of sound, hearing and balance and if we work with healing sounds we can bring back a state of harmony, a more natural healthier resonant frequency. And if I do need to understand the musical side of sound healing I simply ask the musical genius I'd met at nineteen and who is now one of my greatest supporters.

FEEL IT REAL

I've learned that life is just one big orchestral manoeuvre where we are all connected; play the wrong note and disharmony follows. We unconsciously speak in the language of sound and vibration as we feel the `vibes', or do whatever 'sounds' good. I now believe that when we die we simply reside in a different frequency, on a wavelength we can sometimes hear, feel or see when we are 'alive'.

DANCE TO THE RHYTHM OF LIFE

I continue to follow my spirit now. It told me to stop all the therapies, for a while at least, and just feel, so I did. In that time, I learned to dance. I drenched myself in feminine energy, connected to this earthly existence and allowed freedom to simply flow. When you just dance, you feel the music and a sensuality that has nothing to do with your breasts, your hair or your womb but it's how you feel when you connect to the rhythm of life and a mystical melody of sorts.

Sound Healing Therapist.

ABOUT THE AUTHOR

Although trained in many other therapies, Joh is now primarily a Sound Healing Therapist using the transformative power of sound to heal, repair and support others find balance in a chaotic world.

She didn't look for this therapy, it found her in a dream. Ancient knowledge shared and channelled and she can see how life is a melody that sometimes goes out of tune and where the most important relationship to have is with yourself.

Now at the cutting edge of medicine and science, this form of ancient healing is making a resurgence. You re-connect to the rhythm of life and your spirit flows with greater ease. Emotional and physical pain subsides as you simply allow your path to flow with less resistance to change.

CONTACT

http://johjohnson.com/
info@johjohnson.com
https://www.facebook.com/TheArtofSoundTherapy/

PART
THREE

PATIENCE,
SURVIVAL AND
BROKEN DREAMS

KILLING ME SOFTLY WITH
HIS SONG
Kim M. Lovegrove: Australia

*"My philosophy is that not only are you
responsible for your life, but doing the best at
this moment puts you in the best place for the
next moment."*

~ Oprah Winfrey

The scene is a Friday evening at an exclusive restaurant and bar. They came together in the most unlikely of circumstances, but each felt, with great intensity, that from that very first moment, they were meant to be together to the end of time. She had been flying solo for many years, busy working and raising her children, and was now carrying a serious injury that would require further surgery – it could not have been more unexpected. Serendipity had never played a part in her life; but there was no other word for it.

The charismatic musician with gentle, dark features could not take his eyes off her. He had known immediately that she was the mysterious woman that had occupied his thoughts for the last five years. He had been mesmerized by her one night at the private club where he was playing, but she had left before he could meet her. He had not laid eyes on her again until tonight. The difference was that this time he was not going to let her slip away.

She was not looking for a relationship; having survived an extremely acrimonious divorce twelve years earlier, and currently in the midst of a series of painful operations in order to save her leg. Romance and all that comes with it was not on the agenda.

She was out of her wheelchair, but still totally reliant on crutches. That evenings rare excursion out had been kindly arranged, rather spontaneously, by one of her therapists who considered it time she 'got out of the house'.

This is how my love affair began …… full of wonder, amazement, joy and passion. I believe Zac's presence in my life helped me get through my eighth and final operation in much better shape than the previous seven. He visited me every day, and although I needed my sleep, I didn't mind that he would text at all hours of the night to profess his love. To the hopeless romantic in me, everything pointed to the fact that this was finally the man I had been waiting for so long. It was an exciting and glorious feeling, knowing that I was going home after so much time in hospital with a new love in my life. Alas, as I moved into rehabilitation mode and he moved in with me, the relationship soon proved to be an emotional rollercoaster ride – constantly swinging from incredibly amorous highs to painfully heart-wrenching lows. I became vaguely aware that he kept a mysterious secret, but of course I couldn't know exactly what this was.

Zac was a very talented musician and singer, with a long string of reasons and justifications as to why his career had not led him to dizzying heights after one platinum record. He was certainly a big fish in a little pond, in the country town where we lived, and that suited him fine. Nevertheless, it was so special to hear him sing to me at home and dedicate songs to me when he performed.

A strong trait of mine is loyalty and I've learned that while this can be a treasured gift it can also lead to trouble if not paired at least with clear vision. In the very early stages I made a lot of excuses for him. He could always charm me into forgiveness with loving words and beautiful warm hugs. I was making very slow progress with my rehab, but put on a brave face each day and always looked forward to my daily hydrotherapy.

I was unable to drive, so relied on taxis. Strangely, Zac never offered to drive me. He would say that he was very busy doing work on the computer. He lost the one night per week gig where we had met and there were no other opportunities around at that time ... so he said.

He said that he was working on a big development project up north which would put us in a fabulous financial position when complete. 'I' just needed to see us through until 'his ship came in'.

Initially he offered up very little information regarding this development, but soon the story started to unfold in more detail. He even showed me on Google maps where this land was located. Then came the need for him to attend Monday evening dinner meetings in the city and flying trips to the site. None of this made a lot of sense, for a musician, but he was able to rattle off a number of names who would understandably be involved.

It was later that I learned he was leading a double life. I was taking very strong medication for pain so my brain was in a constant fog. The combination of drugs and rose-tinted glasses made life very frustrating for me, as I could not understand how an intelligent woman, like myself, could find herself in such a situation. Whenever, I tried to speak to Zac about stories that he had told me and things that did not stack up, he would become very defensive initially and turn it all around to make me the source of the issue.

Alternatively, he would be very loving and explain what was going on with him in great detail to allay my fears. What I realized much later, was that each time I brought up an issue or confronted him with something that did not make sense, his responses were very elaborate concoctions of something he probably wanted to happen. Yes, he was weaving a very tangled web of lies, which he managed quite well in the beginning. But as time went on, the stress of trying to recall which lie he made up to cover which incident was taking a toll on him and he was no longer the easy going, wonderful man that I had fallen in love with. I found I was anxious all the time. Conversations with him would make my head spin and I felt sucked dry and abused.

A friend tried to tell me that he was a manipulator. This was around the time that someone else informed me that he was still in touch with his previous partner. Before I could speak with him, I happened to see him in the main street sitting in the driver's seat of her car. I moved my crutches very speedily past, but he had seen me. As I was trying to catch my breath in an alcove of the Post Office he surprised me with a kiss and a warm embrace. He had leapt out of the car, leaving her waiting, while he tried to salvage the situation with me. He told me that he loved me and there were reasons that he would explain at home. I already felt like a pretzel, twisting myself inside out just to get through each day with some peace at the end of it, but I continued to try hard to sustain the relationship.

Still in considerable pain, despite my medication, and working very hard at my rehab, I found it enormously taxing trying to think my way out of this mess. I desperately wanted to make sense of the situation. My brain was already tired from my exercises and learning to walk, but I persistently tried to figure him out – a pointless exercise. I learned the hard way.

At that time, I was not aware that it was impossible to work anything out logically with a narcissist. I also tried to help him change from a crazy person. But the more I tried to control this out of control person, in order to have some control of my life, the worse things became. My drug-addled brain became confused with the definition of 'unconditional' love. I would listen to his stories intently, with the hope that we could work things out. From his warped perspective, the way he behaved was everyone else's fault – he was a victim of everyone else and his environment. He blamed, punished, controlled and manipulated because there was 'no-one' home inside himself to do it differently. I still could not comprehend his ability to turn happiness into a nightmare in the blink of an eye.

There had been so many red flags, but I simply was not seeing them. It was a case of the old nursery rhyme: "when he was good he was very, very good and when he was bad he was horrid."

The one thing I did know, however, was that I had to get off the painkillers and make every effort to get my head clear so that I could take responsibility for my own life and the way I was being treated. My surgeon referred me to a renowned Pain Specialist and I explored various alternate modalities. It was a long road to glory!

I began to see with much more clarity, even though I still did not know the entire truth. His jealous outbursts for no reason, knee jerk reactions, tirades about my family and myriad other hurtful barbs would come out of nowhere, totally unwarranted. I came to recognize that this very self-righteous man completely lacked empathy, saying and doing things that were completely unfathomable to me. Despite proposing marriage on three occasions, he simply did not have the consciousness to care about me or my children. He would intentionally ruin special celebrations, particularly Christmas. At these times, he wasn't getting his narcissistic supply of attention so he would create drama or threaten to disappear. Christmas together twice, spent with this narcissist were the saddest and most painful Christmas Days ever for me. I felt that my children would never forgive me for bringing this person into the fold. I felt so totally torn apart.

When I brought up the subject of his financial obligation, yet again, he took great umbrage and, in a split second, became so angry that he threw me across the room like I was a tissue. Taken completely by surprise, I landed on my head, very lucky not to have broken my neck, and momentarily blacked out. It got worse – with a 100kg man sitting on me, pushing my head into a hard floor and hitting me. He left without a key to the apartment building, so I felt safe with some breathing space. Unfortunately, later that night he was granted access when he told a neighbour that he had forgotten his key. I had seen a doctor who encouraged me strongly to make a Police report. I felt a tumult of emotions: terror, emptiness, panic, with shame and guilt at the top of the list, but ultimately it was a false sense of pride and fear of embarrassment that caused me to face it quietly and alone. I didn't know how I could forgive him, but I knew I would try. It wasn't too long before a text from his "ex" set off his hair trigger again. He stormed into the bedroom ripping the covers from the bed, throwing things at me and shouting abuse. When I stood up he went to hit me over the head with a guitar – that's when I called the Police.

I was concerned for my own safety and that of my son. I was also very sensitive to how gossip would affect him, as we lived very close to his school. I chose not to press charges; however, the Constable who came to the scene did lay charges against him. I didn't see Zac again until the court hearing. Even in these circumstances he railed against the lawyers and the Police, blaming 'the system'; but he attempted to charm the female Magistrate and played very sweet with me. It was too late ... I had had enough!

Although my leg still caused me considerable pain and I was still healing from the trauma of the accident and multiple surgeries, I was very hard on myself. I was devastated emotionally, physically and financially and kicking myself for letting it happen. I was a smart, strong, courageous woman, yet I had been manipulated and conned from the outset. But worst of all was the guilt I felt with regard to my children. I had tried to shield them as much as possible but it became impossible to hide the reality, particularly when, during one rampage he had demanded that I choose between my daughter and him. Once the betrayal was fully revealed, there was a lot of psychic catching up to do in order to get current with what was REALLY real, rather than what I thought was real. Yes, it took me a while to see the light, but thankfully I did eventually.

I felt almost destroyed, yet I have not let it destroy me. I had to learn to take back my personal power and become self-generative. I had more healing to do – I had to go inside and heal the real unconscious reasons and wounds that had allowed me to stay attached to this abusive man and which had prevented me from pulling away sooner. Since I was a very small girl I had yearned for love, security, safety and stability; I knew now that I had to stop looking fruitlessly outside of myself for these things.

The gift from this terribly toxic three-year relationship is that I went on a journey inside to discover emotional peace and wholeness. Initially, I was filled with a sense of failure and futility and an inability to trust myself to make good choices. But I learned to love myself and forgive myself and open my heart again to the absolute joy that love brings.

Since that fateful ending, I have been blessed to meet some wonderful people who have helped me along the way to welcoming my new life. A most beautiful man appeared in my life not too long after, someone with integrity, quiet strength, good looks and intelligence. He is powerful, yet kind and generous towards everyone. He displays a willingness to support me in every way he can and he is understanding and empathetic. This is a man I had never even dreamed existed, yet he walked straight into my world with no big announcement or fanfare. Herein, is the next lesson – to never give up or give in .... feel the love inside you first and the Universe will ensure that when the time is right, probably when you least expect it, the person who is a perfect match and fit for you will appear. We must trust that everything happens for a reason, and sometimes that can be hard to accept. I have learned to look for the gift in every situation, sometimes it takes a while to see it, but it is always there. So, I can now look back on those three years and appreciate their role in leading me to a different path and all the joy that I have found along the way. Through that experience I learned so much about life, love and myself. And I now know the joy of dreaming BIG!

'Our wounds are often the openings into the best and most beautiful part of us.'~ David Richo

ABOUT THE AUTHOR

Having honed her leadership skills throughout her Army career, Kim moved into a completely different arena following years of study and research in the fields of alternate medicine/therapies and coaching.

She has confronted many challenges in her personal life, working through limiting beliefs and overcoming more than her fair share of trauma and relationship and health issues. She threw herself further into medical research when doctors and top ranking specialists gave up on her baby son. (He is now a healthy, handsome twenty-year old, elite athlete.) She again defied medical diagnosis, learned to walk again after a serious accident. Doctors had advised that she was lucky to still have her right leg, but she wouldn't walk again. The lessons, learnings and wisdom that she has gleaned from her own life journey only enhance her ability to connect with people, and truly benefit her coaching clients.

Her passion, and where she excels, is working as a Results Coach, assisting people to reach their full potential and ultimately their innermost desires.

CONTACT

Email: kimmlovegrove@gmail.com
Skype: Charlotte India 007

A STEPMOTHER'S TALE
Caroline Newman: London

*"The people we are in relationship with are
always a mirror, reflecting our own beliefs,
and simultaneously we are mirrors, reflecting
their beliefs. So... relationship is one of the most
powerful tools for growth".*

~ Shakti Gawain

My name is Caroline and I am a stepmother. I am part of a stepfamily. Today we have all reached a place of getting along. We have learned to compromise and we have found common ground. But it was not always this way. Let me tell you a little bit more about my journey.

When I started writing this chapter, it was my intention to vent my spleen; to tell my story to warn others in the same situation, so to speak. It was intended to be my story and all about me.

I had only considered this whole saga from my perspective. But as I began to truly reflect on what has happened over the last 6 years, I felt ashamed. I realised that I had not truly stepped outside of my story.

As a life coach, I have helped people have breakthroughs in relationships using the tools and strategies that I had spent years studying. But when it came to helping myself, I found it hard to self-coach.

It has not been easy. Arguments, jealousies and resentments were common in our changed family. We became a family with a different shape to the one people think of as 'normal'.

BEING A STEPMUM

It's hard being a step mum. I got caught up in a cycle of anger and bitterness and it seemed impossible to make changes.

I felt helpless in the face of my own emotions and powerless to alter the feelings of those around me.

I have often felt tempted to throw in the towel and run away because it was too terrible and I didn't know what to do.

I often felt like I was drowning. I felt that I couldn't see the whole picture. I knew that the problems with my partner's children were not just to do with me and my children. It had a great deal to do with the past and what had got us to where we were.

I tried hard to understand the effect of the past on the present. I tried to find a solution to the problem without being exactly sure what the real problem was.

I alienated myself from my family and my friends because I didn't want them to know how bad things had gotten. I racked my brain and searched my soul daily. It affected my eating habits. I went from being healthy to overweight.

It was exhausting. But I survived by looking forward to how it could be if things were different.

I woke up every day looking at the misery we were experiencing. And yes, of course I felt like walking away many times. But I knew this was not the solution. I just didn't know how to get from where I was to where I wanted to be.

I am a life coach for goodness sake. This is what I do. I help people solve their problems. But I was in a state of despair.

I started to blame my partner's eldest son for all our problems. Then I blamed my partner for not supporting me or taking my side. I took on the role of victim. I blamed him for not treating me with respect and insisting that his children respect me. I didn't appreciate the impossible situation that he was in.

DIVORCE

When I got divorced, my ex-husband was angry when he saw our children having contact with my new partner.

My ex-husband and his new partner went on to have a child together so that brought up all kinds of stuff for me and our children. The only person who appeared immune to all the tension was his new baby son, who just embraced everyone.

I often think how lovely it would be to be that innocent again, or if it is even possible for adults who have suffered the stress associated with the 6 D's: Death, Divorce, Disappointment, Debt, Displacement and Disease. If only we could go back to that state of innocence.

The complexities and pressures became compounded when my children came to visit. His children rejected them. My children were keen to try and make it work for my sake, but when they felt the resistance they too withdrew and gave up trying. Once again, I felt like I was the only one working to keep everyone together.

I found that in our divorce and re-partnering, the leftover baggage from previous relationships led to misunderstandings, resentment and hurt.

LOSS

Our families changed because of loss. My partner's wife died. He lost her.

Our children had to face and resolve things which they did not choose; that were outside their control.

For me and their dad it was a new start, but for them it was a tragic ending. It highlighted for them that things would never be the same again. A reminder of the tragedy of their mother's passing.

What they needed was predictability. For both their parents to be available to show them love and to be valued.

A parent is for life. A partner is not. Whether married or not.

The children felt abandoned, rejected and guilty. So how did they respond to their Daddy moving on without consulting them? They resorted to self-destructive ways of getting control, and showed their pain at being left out.

At first, they tried hard to pretend that the changes didn't matter. Their behaviour fluctuated between silence, sulking, turning their friends and family against me and trying to make me feel less worthy. Then the passive aggressive behaviour turned into slamming doors. They became disrespectful, mean and insulting.

Then the floodgates opened, meanness, bullying, silent treatment, leaving the room when I came in. They had unfinished business and boy did they let us know it.

My partner also struggled to come to terms with his wife's death. This influenced the new family we were trying to form.

BRINGING FAMILIES TOGETHER

What a mess I have made of my life and my children's lives by the choices I have made. These were ignorant and selfish choices. I hope and pray that our children make better choices.

I was abandoned as a child and since then have had an overwhelming need to belong.

When my partner asked me to be his partner after struggling on his own after the death of his wife, I was seen as the answer, a refuge. He wasn't coping well on his own. But he really wasn't ready for me and our relationship.

Having me around was comforting and painful at the same time. He didn't intend for us to form a new family. But he wanted me to get on with his children and help him look after them. He wanted me to fill the gap in his life, but not be a stepmother.

His children had lost their mother and found some consolation in being useful to their dad and being protective of each other. Their father would discuss with them the things he used to discuss with his wife. They had made joint decisions about the home and the family together. Yet they were not consulted about him starting a new relationship.

We were jealous of each other and each other's place in their Dad's and my partner's life. My partner felt under extreme pressure to try and please everyone and to manage the situation. I had to juggle arrangements and our living arrangements became complex.

BEING 'DIFFERENT'

We all want to fit in and belong. Society's view of what it means to be a member of a family gives us plenty of reasons to want to avoid being in a stepfamily. No one wants to be seen as a failure. In fact, many people have a fear of failure. Few of us want to be seen as different. Children and teenagers in particular don't want to be seen as different. They often do everything they can to fit in and to be the same as their friends.

People view 'different' families as dangerous, anti-social, dysfunctional, threatening.

For many years, people in the traditional nuclear family feared "single parent" families. Now people seem to fear families that change and reform. It would appear that even those people who are part of 'different' families fear those who are in different families to their own. How do you feel about same sex parents? Women who use a sperm bank in order to become a mother and never know the father of their child?

Childless families? Are they even a real "family"? Do you see how your own prejudices come into play?

DIFFERENT IS THE NEW NORMAL

It used to be, "them" normal; "us" different. Nowadays, different is the "new" normal. You are as likely to come across a "different" family as you are a traditional, nuclear family.

But there is still a society wide effort to keep the idea of family change as exceptional and abnormal.

People who are in unhappy or in stale relationships may see step families as a threat. People would refer to us as "new lovers"; "young love" with a sense of longing as they contemplated their stale relationships. They wouldn't, of course, want to go through the pain of bereavement or divorce to get the fresh start or find a new love. Human beings are a strange dichotomy.

Is it because one partner senses that the other might start to get ideas about fresh start? When one member of a group gets divorced, sometimes the other husbands or wives in the group might consider following suit. The cracks in their relationships might become exposed.

At the time, I sensed jealousy from women who had no children of their own. It felt like not only had I got my own children, I had now acquired additional children as well as a new husband.

So, I struggled to come to terms with my own feelings and my partner's insecurities. I felt I was blamed for everything. I felt defensive, angry, and resentful of my partner for not being more supportive. I believed that I was guilty and I was to blame for loving their dad, brother, uncle; everyone else closed ranks against me. If they could have blamed me for the death they would have.

I blamed my partner for not standing up for me; for not setting proper moral standards; for overcompensating. I believed he blamed himself for his wife and his children's mother dying. I felt guilty for moving on to a new relationship, for finding new love.

When my marriage went wrong, both of us had an equal responsibility to deal with the fallout and the anger and pain. We had a responsibility to help our children, yet we used them as weapons in our continuing battle. At first I chose to complain to anyone who would listen about how awful my step children were and how their family were treating me. I inadvertently became the victim and made him the villain.

THE TURNING POINT

Finally, I decided to deal with what life threw at me. I chose to cast myself in a different role. I would no longer be the victim. I would be the leader that I know I am meant to be. I chose to love instead of judge. I learned to accept. I accepted myself. I accepted the situation I was in. I accepted my stepsons. I accepted that things are not perfect and never will be perfect.

I remembered that I had choice. In this situation, I could choose to be a duck or an eagle. If you get up in the morning expecting to have a bad day, you'll rarely disappoint yourself. Ducks quack and complain. Eagles soar above the crowd. I realised that I was always quacking and complaining, so I decided to change my attitude and become an eagle. This powerful choice I made transformed every area of my life.

I reminded myself that I had chosen this. So, I decided to GET REAL:

- Grow in Grace
- Enrol others
- Trust myself, the process and others
- Reach out and ask for help
- Engage in a meaningful way
- Accept the situation
- Love myself and others

This is how I've been able to go through the rollercoaster that has been my life; since I said, "yes", to starting a relationship with a widower and his two young sons.

I have failed many times, yet each time I have tried to fail forward. I took the lesson. I made adjustments. I picked myself up. I affirmed myself and I continued.

FAILING FORWARD

Many human beings fear failure. We are not prepared for it. We have an image of a perfect life. Social media compels us to project an image of success. To pretend that we have it altogether. When we fail, we feel scared and out of control.

But we will all fail at some time. Even the most successful relationships have conflicts and problems. The best relationships are made by overcoming difficulties and coming to understandings and compromise. Would you rather have a step family or relationship where people argue and have disagreements, or where people are scared to speak their minds or confront their fears?

My motto has always been, "Better Out Than In", meaning that it's best to say what's on your mind rather than bottle it up. That is how I've managed in life and succeeded in my relationship.

SOLUTIONS

Here is a summary of the solutions that I found helpful during my journey. I hope they help you:

- Pray
- Visualise what you want
- Manage your emotions
- Have a solid support network - join or

create a loving, sharing environment of people with similar issues, or people who will listen without judgement

- Take time out to rest and take care of yourself every day
- Know yourself. Sun Sui said, "Know yourself and know your enemy and in a thousand battles you'll have a thousand victories".
- Accept that it may take months or even years to get from one stage to another
- Set goals for all areas of your life, including your relationships
- Sometimes you have to let go of what you want and hold on to what you need
- Strive for self-improvement: You cannot solve a problem with the level of knowledge that created the problem
- Accept what is and create new possibilities

CONCLUSION

Families come in all shapes and sizes and are continuously changing. We need to embrace all families, and love ourselves and our children. Families are one of the best places to find love and connection. It may be a different love to what you were expecting based on the box you have been encouraged to put love into.

But it's time to *unbox love.*

Love is important. Families are important. They are one of the best ways for caring for each other, getting your needs met and meeting the needs of others. It is also normal for the form of a family to vary and be diverse. What matters is that children and adults become members of a group that cares for them, values them and supports them. The shape and name of that group is less important than the way it holds you and looks after you.

ABOUT THE AUTHOR

Caroline is an international trainer, successful business woman in the fields of law and people development. She is also an author, business consultant, transformational coach, a professional actor, TV presenter and facilitator. Her aim is to establish practices such as work/life balance, positive thinking, activity management as a way of life to promote good health, improved relationships and better quality of life for everyone.

Caroline has created two successful award winning businesses, and now lives the life she dreamed about, is a credible example of work-life balance, an ambassador for living life fully and a strong role model for other women.

Caroline has 2 sons and 2 stepsons. They are all smart, wonderful young men. Caroline founded the African Women Lawyers' Association and the annual Women of the African Diaspora Leadership Conference. She does a lot of charity work and was Trustee of the Howard League for over 15 years, Vice-Chair of its Law Management Committee, member of the Law Society's Council.

Caroline enjoys keeping fit by working out and dancing. She loves to ski and to travel, especially to warm climates.

CONTACT:

Email: caroline@caroline-newman.com
Website: http://www.caroline-newman.com
Twitter: https://twitter.com/carolinenewman1
Facebook: Caroline Newman
LinkedIn: Caroline Newman

MY AUTHENTIC LOVE
Julia Keller: London

*"Today I choose life. Every morning when I wake up
I can choose joy, happiness, negativity, pain... To feel
the freedom that comes from being able to continue
to make mistakes and choices - today I choose to feel
life, not to deny my humanity but embrace it."*

~ *K. Aucoin*

ONCE UPON A TIME

My own love story began when I was still a little girl. Even then I loved the idea of love, my mind filled with fairy tales and stories of women being rescued by a handsome prince. My imagination was full of scenarios of how my own love story would unfold someday when some handsome prince would arrive, rescuing me from a ho-hum existence, and take me to be his bride in his beautiful palace. He would make sure that I felt adored and cared for, and every single day of my existence would be full of exciting activities.

Let me just say that real life does not always turn out quite like we fantasize as young girls. I began running auditions for some amazing guys to fulfil the role of "Handsome Prince" early in my life, as I started dating when I was thirteen. I had more boyfriends than a girl probably needed, but none of these suitors matched my imagined criteria. Something was always missing, which meant I became incredibly skilled at walking away with as little personal damage as possible.

It worked until I fell in love in my early twenties. The feeling of love was so unforeseen and unusual that it hit me like an unexpected bomb exploding: full of passion and excitement, mixed with anticipation and anxiety. I began to believe that maybe this thing called "love" was something that would never happen for me, as I was unable to find that person that could fill me with that elusive sensation. This is not a statement that sounds very encouraging from a woman who years later is now teaching "love" to others as a Love Coach.

I was around the age of twenty-two when this emotion called "love" decided to knock on my door. It came in the form of a relationship which had all the necessary ingredients of a perfect ill-fated romance novel. Despite both our best efforts, circumstance and obstacles worked against us, leaving my heart raw and desperate to satisfy a craving it so yearned to fill.

My search began in earnest. I wanted to feel that alive again, that in need, that desired. I felt the necessity of love for the first time; like a vessel longing to be filled. What I wanted was an enduring love, one that would not fade. I dreamed of happy endings and learned to twist and turn men to squeeze the love that I needed out of them. But I had not learned yet the importance of working to improve yourself, so I still would run away the minute imperfection reared its' ugly face or any kind of crisis appeared (even if it was minor), as I then considered the relationship ill-fated.

MY PRINCE ARRIVES

Eventually, the man who was to become my first husband arrived in my life. I knew immediately when I met him, to the extent that I even called and told my mother that I had, at last, met the man that would be my husband one day. I think my mother was more surprised than me as she was thinking that there was no man that would ever reach the bar I had set.

I was twenty-five then and thought I knew exactly what I wanted. I had experienced enough men to recognise quality when I found it.

Just before I had met my husband, I decided a different approach was needed, so I created a list and meditated on it. I would visualize the man I desired.

It was a complete surprise to me that within a very short-time of visualizing him, he became a reality. I knew he was a keeper instantly. I had to make sure he did not slip through my fingers like sand escaping, so I handed him a deadline early. I just expected that all would go as I planned and wanted eventually.

Despite our perpetual ups and downs, our relationship did move forward. He chose to propose rather than to lose me, so he became my first husband. He was the first man who stopped me from walking away. With every down, I would consider running, but somehow the love we felt for each other kept us together; well it did in the early years.

Less than a decade later, we had become a young family with children, but the tensions in our relationship seem greater than ever. Although we tried to be a couple, we always seemed at odds with each other. My husband ticked all of the boxes on my list. He was handsome, charming, intelligent and a great provider. So why did I feel so unfulfilled in our marriage?

I learned an important lesson about lists: be careful what you wish for as you may just get exactly what you ordered.

The thing is, what was missing in our relationship was precisely the items left off my list. I have perfected my insight into list creation since then into a most miraculous process, supported with effective techniques, which have enabled me to grow my brand as a Love Coach and an impressive list of satisfied clients.

The constant disagreements and perpetual misunderstandings forced me into deciding it was best to run again, so I told my husband I was leaving him, believing that I'd find something better, or maybe at least some peace away from our rocky existence.

Although my new life looked an improvement from my previous perspective, and I felt able to relax again, as I hadn't for a long time in my marriage, the reality was far different. My life had deteriorated to a low point of loneliness and unhappiness when I decided to pray to whatever higher power for help, and a light shined in my direction.

I was running in a park near my home (not something I normally chose to do). I could hardly see my way as the tears of sorrow flowed down my cheeks. I cried for my loneliness, for my lost dreams, for everything that had not gone as planned, and for the feeling of not knowing what I was doing or what I was meant for. With my eyes blinded I could not see where I was heading in my run or in my life.

THE PRINCE FINDS A NEW PRINCESS

A few years after our divorce my now ex-husband met the perfect woman for him. She was sweet and nice to be around; even I enjoyed her company and liked her kids, who my own kids became good friends with.

My ex-husband had found his loving relationship: a second chance at love; and I wished for my second chance too.

It was the first time that I really took stock of why so many of my relationships hadn't worked up to now: perhaps the problem was me. Did I call it quits too soon? Did my search for perfection in love put me in danger of ending up alone? Surely there was a balance between leaving too quickly and staying too long; but had I actually found it? Had I given up too soon every time?

When such a realization hits you, it comes hard and takes your breath away. It threatens to undermine and destroy your whole perspective of yourself. But, most of all, if you accept it for the gift that it is, it breaks you in the necessary way to help you rebuild again, this time a better version of who you once were.

With tears streaming down my face, I begged the universe (or whatever higher power was out there) to hear me. I needed a guide to show me the way. What was my destiny? Surely it cannot just be a trail of broken relationships.

AND THEN THE PENNY DROPPED

It was as if a big secret had been revealed to me. Now I knew what I needed to do to earn the life that I wanted.

My work began. First, and most importantly, I took a short break from men. I decided to focus my energies on me. I wanted to understand love and relationships better, so I began studying and reading what the experts had to say. What I found was that by focusing on me with the same enthusiasm as I had on attracting men, my ideal life started to materialize. Finally, my life began to improve and to shape into what I'd always wanted.

I was not actively looking for love, but my belief in it materializing was unwavering. Now being happy with who I was, I knew that I'd meet someone amazing eventually. I met someone who initially seemed like the sort of person I would like. He was in fact, not the partner I needed for long-term, but, as it turned out, he helped to move my life in a new direction. Our relationship was fun and exciting, but now I had two kids, and I didn't see us becoming a cohesive family unit.

But something happened that was different. Before I left, he gave me the most incredible gift of all. It was this man who convinced me to pursue the one career I had always wanted, but never thought possible: he persuaded me to become a Love Coach.

A LIFETIME VOCATION REALISED

It made sense of course. I had always advised others on what to do to improve their own love life and even had several marriages credited to my matchmaking and advise skills.

I had read about as many books about love as anyone out there and asked countless successful couples, women who seemed to know how to capture the hearts of men, and men who seemed to understand what women should do better for their advice.

I did research on love without even being asked to; it had always been my favourite topic of discussion. I had even studied Psychology in University with my focus being Attraction and Relationships. So why not make it into a career?

My new boyfriend funded the beginning of my enterprise and even made it possible for me to work with the Coach who started me in the right direction. Then I signed my first client and was the force behind her incredible story of transformation. It was the start of a path forward that I haven't looked back from. I studied Coaching, NLP, and now Hypnotherapy: all in an effort to help my clients better in whatever way would work best for them.

MY OWN LIFE STORY

My own love story improved as well. In the process of all of this self-work and the positive energy of finally uncovering my life's path, I also began to meet the kind of men that I really wanted. After several short relationships with men who didn't completely fit, I eventually met someone who did. He is attractive, kind, intelligent, giving, and a great father to his little girl (and lovely with my kids too); our chemistry is also pretty great and we've had a wonderful and harmonious time together.

Thanks to him, I thrived in my life and a comfort level became established; he thrived too. I finished my first book (Attract Authentic Love) which is being published and will be out in bookstores in the Summer, and his career picked up again. We both became more fit together and our kids get along. It seemed perfect, except that I write this after a difficult patch (and some deep discussion) which leaves me needing to decide which way to go.

I love this man greatly; but I love myself more.

All of the self-work that I've done brought me to a point where I know exactly what I want now and what I'm ready for. I teach the women that I work with that you have to love yourself first and then you share that love with the special people in your life. But you can't share love that you don't have just as you can't compromise on everything you believe in just because someone you love asks that of you.

So, we've come to a fork in the road where I have to question the importance of my own belief system and choose between what I want for my life going forward and the man that I love. I would teach the women that I work with to choose themselves first and not stay in something that possibly will never be exactly what they want because of fear of not finding something else. So what advice will I give to myself?

My own personal love story is yet unfinished. At the moment of writing this, I stand at a crossroads of love and I don't yet know which way it will go.

Over the course of my story, I've felt heartache and pain and passion and incredible love. The main thing I can say is that I have lived love to the full.

It was only when I set my heart free to love that I was able to feel that love come to me. Our hearts must have wings to soar in order to reach incredible heights.

The biggest learning, however, was that the great love I sought I had to find within myself first.

There would never be anyone capable of fulfilling me unless I was able to fulfil myself. No one could ever love us enough to make up for love that we don't already hold for ourselves. We have to find self-love first before looking to receive it from someone else.

And as far as that fantasy of that prince that was supposed to rescue me and satisfy all of my needs: well, after more than two decades of searching, I've finally realized that maybe the only person who can really rescue me is me. I have all of the means within to realize real dreams by believing and by moving towards them.

That's what I teach my clients after all: we have the ability to create and control our own destiny. We don't need to be rescued by anyone else because we can be our own rescuer.

That's not to say that we don't ask for help; quite the opposite. I ask for help all of the time, and I usually receive it.

I still believe in happily ever after, but I believe that it is up to us to work towards it. It is up to us to create that ideal love story and that ideal relationship that we dream of and hope for. Everything we need to make it happen is within us. Sometimes we need a bit of help and that's ok. That's why I'm there to help my clients keep moving forward; and that's why I have my own coach to help me.

But, in the end, the real movement is up to us. We are, after all, the only true writers of our own ideal story.

ABOUT THE AUTHOR

Julia Keller is a Transformational Love Coach who empowers women and men serious about improving their love life to be the writer of their ideal love story by finding, claiming, and improving true love. Julia has a BA in Psychology and an MBA and has studied Coaching, NLP, and Hypnotherapy.

Julia's journey began with her own personal failure when she joined the unhappy statistics after her divorce. Because she'd witnessed enough couples who were happily in love, even though occasional struggles, she knew that love could last and that we all deserve to find that special someone who adores and accepts us just as we are. What followed was a series of first-hand interviews with anyone who would answer her questions about love, dating, and relationships and a series of interviews on YouTube (search Honest Conversations Julia Keller) and on her blog (http://www.juliakeller.co.uk).

CONTACT

Twitter: https://twitter.com/JuliaKellerUK
Facebook and Instagram: @coachjuliakeller
YouTube: Julia Keller Coaching

A SYMBOLIC REFLECTION
Cherron Lee Johnson: London

*'By three methods we may learn wisdom:
First, by reflection, which is noblest; Second,
by imitation, which is easiest; and third by
experience, which is the bitterest."*

~ Confucius

THE CATALYST

That night was about me shutting the door, running a hot bubbly bath watching mindless TV and pampering myself after a hard day of essays, deadlines and exhibitions, working on my Master's Degree in Art and Design at University, this was a mini reward to myself. Me time, down time, my time.

I could see the television in the kitchen through the bathroom door. I believe it was a Tuesday night about 7.30pm in 1994. I remember feeling settled. It was my time to breathe, and, just be.

Then suddenly, something happened. I had no idea what, but something did just happen.

From that moment on everything was different, not just different in the ordinary sense but in an extraordinary way. There was a stillness in the air, and a distance between myself and this space and the environment. It felt weird.

What *it* was, I do not know.......... my brain couldn't quite fathom what.

That period of "in-between-ness" seemed to have held me in abeyance. This twilight zone was quiet, peaceful and gentle. In this suspension of time, if time existed at all....... everything just was.

Gradually my visual senses awakened. My eyes started to scan the scene in slow motion like a detective's torch light in a movie, looking for evidence to unravel the mystery.

I started roaming in the kitchen, the furthest point away from my body and gradually into the passage then entering into the bathroom. Was I dreaming or just observing? I had to recalculate, reconfigure and re-equate myself with this space time existence. Everything was familiar, but strange. I could hear the sound of distant chatter which was coming from the TV, which gradually grew a bit more audible as my attention re-engaged.

There was a missing link between a time before that *thing* that happened and my consciousness thereafter.

So I was in the bathroom in the bath, ok I get it and I was still there. The bath water was warm and waist height. I was facing in the direction of the TV. There seemed to be a lot of stuff in the bath……. I soon came to realise……

it was glass.

The bath was full of broken glass.

The jagged shapes glistened as they floated on top of the water. Some tinged with my blood. Different shapes, different sizes. I even captured fractions of my reflection. This cascade of shiny objects had a beauty about it. It was as if I had become a part of an art installation, one I would have created while at Central School of Art way back when as a teenager.

What an inconvenient time to have an accident. Seriously? How and when did that happen?

I started to examine my body. I looked at my arm and all I could see was about 12 inches of my skin sliced and hanging down exposing red raw flesh. In that one moment, my first thought was very clear and blunt, "that looks like meat displayed in the butcher's shop."

I felt totally separated from my body. My body was something I housed. My body was not the essence of me, nor my consciousness, nor that which makes me, me.

I got it. I was not in my body. I felt a part of a profound calm frequency. It was awesome, something very divine, a different state of existence.

As my consciousness started to anchor back in my body, time seemed to speed up. I gradually became aware of what had happened and the TV was no longer a distant chatter, I could hear it at normal volume. From that moment on precisely, I began to feel pain.

The big black framed mirror above the bath had fallen on me. It measured the width of the bath and almost the height up to the ceiling. I bet I am the only person to say a soap opera saved their life. I was lucky. Imagine if my body was positioned another way? I won't go there.

The challenge I now faced was how to get out of the bath safely and get to the phone. I had to do it.

I just got a glimpse of a me connected to a purity, my soul, my spirit, that something I always read about. I just experienced my mind and soul detached from my body. I had to muster inner power, that eternal me that I now know exists to get my body to move and get help.

I somehow got to the phone in the next room but lacked the strength and co-ordination to dial the number. My finger slipped on the redial which was my saving grace. I had dialled my cousin's number. He had just walked into his house, timing was perfect. He called the ambulance and rushed over.

My cousin promptly arrived just before the ambulance. I felt safe and in good hands.

The other hero of the night was the compassionate ambulance man. I completely forgot my face was covered in a bright blue facemask and this angel offered to remove the mask before I ventured outside the house. He tenderly wiped my face clean.

I remember finding this funny, it hurt to smile. He wanted to save me from embarrassment as I would be sat in A&E...... probably for a while. My cousin helped me to get dressed. I was then lifted into the ambulance on a stretcher fully clothed with smooth glowing skin.

IN THE BEGINNING

The story really began seven years before.

I had been travelling for a year having wonderful adventures across the globe. This abruptly came to an end when I found a lump in my breast. My immediate response was to come home. This lump turned out to be benign. However, I came back to London disorientated and vulnerable. I went to a night club and met a guy. This was quite a whirlwind romance. He swept me off my feet, showered me with gifts and attention. Next thing I knew I was living in his flat.

He was an entrepreneur busy creating his empire. I loved his fire, energy and maverick attitude. This I could see was a reflection of what I wanted back for myself but at that time was lacking. I just spent one year of being courageous and travelling, seeing new sights, doing new things, meeting new people and making my own rules fearlessly.

I had no idea I was entering his world of chaos, bankruptcy and insecurity until after a few months when I was living in his flat. He hid it well.

He was a gentle guy starting to lose control, he became increasingly angry, irrational and impossible to live with.

How the hell had I arrived at that point? Scooped up in his mess that was obviously going on before I entered the scene. I was a distraction for him not to face up to deal with his life crumbling.

I had to get out of this situation. It was unhealthy and miserable for me.

I didn't want to accept the relationship was doomed. Instead, I chose to hide behind his hell because I felt sorry for him, the wounded child and life's a bitch story. He could not take responsibility; he was in a spiral of despair. I wanted to help but it was impossible as I didn't know what was really going on. This went on for six months.

One day after work I arrived back at the flat to find it all boarded up and an eviction notice and crew there. In my naivety, I didn't even know back then that these things happened, let alone to people I was involved with.

BLESSINGS COME IN ALL DISGUISES. THANK YOU, UNIVERSE.

I explained I had my personal belongings in there. I was given a date and time that I could go back and collect them.

That day came and I grabbed all my gear into a taxi. His mum was there and said that he would not be coming and that I could take anything I wanted. I did call him a coward plus many harsher words but I now can see he was having a nervous breakdown. So, I collected my things and took the large black framed mirror that he had actually made with his own hands. That mirror travelled with me to my mum's, and two homes later and I never saw him again.

I hung that mirror in my bathroom. I liked to do most things myself. I loved being the DIY queen, I sanded floors and built my own wardrobes so putting up a mirror was a piece of cake.

Seven years later this happened. My seven years of bad luck was really before the mirror broke because every time I looked in it there was always a memory logged in the back of my mind.

Unconsciously I was allowing him to remain in my life. I was still angered. I did not make that connection previously how a piece of furniture could hold his energy, his vibration, all ingrained in that object. All those memories, his pain, all the sadness I had allowed this into my sacred space. But.... Why not? I had a big mirror that looked very grand in my Victorian home.

The *accident* was really a wakeup call and turned out to be a most precious gift of an awakening for me. Particularly, as I didn't take the first cue after the eviction notice and just cut all ties!

REFLECTIONS

Every time I now look at my scar, I smile within and it doesn't hurt anymore. It serves as a reminder of the infinite divine me housed in this body. I take ownership of both the *I* and my body. I can walk tall because the *I* is magnificent so that makes my physical home, my body magnificent too.

I have no choice but to embrace this as I don't need another painful lesson to push me into alignment. We will always get challenges but there are degrees of challenges and I am responsible for how I respond.

This experience served as a major catalyst to my personal expansion and growth.

For me, this was not just about being aware of my higher consciousness but having a balance in everything, between both the spiritual and earthly reality and how I can apply it. Understanding the union of mind, body and spirit and how they are interconnected. To learn more and to tap into what feels authentic to become more intuitive. To be in stride with my rhythm and flow, I endeavour to live my life on my terms, with no regrets and without hurting anyone.

It has to start with me!

The best weapon of defence is to love yourself. It is my responsibility to feel complete and love myself before I enter a relationship of any sort. There is always someone out there happy to fill in your inadequacies.......... but then, fill it with what?

This has taught me to always take the time to reflect in the mirror of my soul. Call it meditation or just me time.

I remember as a child we had a tabby kitten and we put him in front of a large mirror and observed his reaction.

He was confused. He thought he had a new friend but could not touch and feel this friend. He was challenged and disturbed about this other being staring directly at him, following him, doing everything he was doing but still had no real connection. Confusion turned into annoyance, which then turned into frustration because he did not realise he had the control.

The next question then could be "what is it we choose to see?" That depends on so many factors particularly as our brain registers billions of pieces of information per second! Ways of seeing can always change but what never changes for me is the context that I frame myself in, which is *I am a spiritual being having a human experience.*

I want to continue to live life fearlessly, make decisions outside the box, step more into that feminine energy of creation. Dance when I want to and how I want to even if someone is watching and don't care. Know when to say yes or no and mean it. Smile or shout when it feels right. Swagger gracefully in my Goddess high heels and feel gloriously graceful or slob out and feel equally comfortable with that when I need to as well.

I suppose this is about making decisions and not sitting on the fence to have life make the decisions for you. Even if it may appear to be a wrong move, there's a lesson there somewhere. So maybe there is no such thing as a mistake.

EMPOWERMENT THROUGH REFLECTION

Two main lessons this experience has taught me.

Firstly, do not hold on to stuff that holds bad memories, detach from those energies and then you can choose how you want to respond to them.

Secondly, our bodies are temporary homes, so love, connect and respect it.

This is why I trained in Theta Healing and practice Reiki, an ancient energy system of healing that helps bring harmony and balance within and around us. In addition to this, I teach Pilates as a tool for facilitating mindfulness. The six main principles of Pilates offer an integrative approach of mind, body and spirit to exercise. They are based on centring, concentration, control, precision, breath and flow. This helps you work from the inside out to create balance and transformation while operating from a place of integrity. As a result, you move with grace and poise from a powerful core centre elegantly empowered.

Most of all I want to be a source of inspiration to my daughter and her wonderful father.

We are all on this journey of life, hopefully evolving as we live more consciously. Therefore, what may seem like a mistake can also be your biggest lesson to serve you and to help you be of any value to others.

ABOUT THE AUTHOR

Cherron is a Pilates Teacher and a Reiki Master. With 25 years in the Fitness and Wellness industry Cherron has worked with thousands of clients in classes, workshops, retreats and private sessions.

Cherron's story takes you on a journey of conscious awakening. This is echoed in her work, helping her clients to feel enriched and inspired by gaining understanding on how their mind, body and breath work in unison creating transformation from the inside out.

With a background in dance, this adds a unique element to her practice. This helps enable her clients to move with grace and poise from a strong core centre and a toned body feeling elegantly empowered.

Download Your Free EBook *"'How To Feel better Naked over 40'*

http://www.cherronleejohnson.com/naked/

CONTACT

http://www.cherronleejohnson.com
Info@cherronleejohnson.com

DRASTIC STEPS FOR LOVE
Toni Harris Taylor: USA

"To succeed in life, you need three things: a wishbone, a backbone and a funny bone."

~ Reba McEntire

NOT QUITE MY FIRST LOVE!

"You're pregnant," the nurse said in a calm voice. I stared at her. "What did you say?" She repeated the words that would change the trajectory of my life forever. "You're pregnant." I said, "Are you sure?"

She said, "Yes, I'm positive, you're positive." Wow, silly me. I thought I couldn't get pregnant. After all, I had been sexually active for several years and nothing, so I thought it wasn't possible for me to get pregnant.

I guess I was wrong. I was 22 years old and pregnant by a married man; not my married man, but one belonging to someone else. Fortunately, I had come to my senses and broke it off with him already, but obviously not quick enough. Now I was pregnant. What was I going to do? I considered abortion, adoption, suicide (I can be a little dramatic), and finally, keeping my baby. I decided to keep my baby and to raise him by myself.

BIG BRANDON

My best friend at the time invited me to get out of the house and attend a barbeque for Labour Day. There was a guy on her job who liked her and he invited her to attend. I needed to get out of my slump so I attended with her.

She introduced me to her friend. "Toni, this is Brandon. Brandon, this is Toni."

"Nice to meet you," I said. To make a long story short, somehow Brandon and I became friends.

He would talk to me about my friend and how she wouldn't give him the time of day (she said he was too big for her because he weighed over 300 pounds). He became my friend throughout my pregnancy.

I shared with him my concerns with being a single mother and he listened. We grew closer and closer. Although I didn't have that passionate love for him, I truly loved him as a friend and a good person. Six months after we met, we were married. My first drastic step for REAL love. As in any typical marriage, Brandon and I went through many ups and downs.

In 2007, we were going through some particularly hard times and I wanted out of the marriage. I felt I had outgrown him. I walked away from our eighteen-year marriage. Something I regret to this day.

SINGLE AGAIN

Brandon became very bitter. He allowed other people to influence his actions. Because I was the primary breadwinner, he went after his "half" and got it. I paid financially and emotionally in the divorce. It got real ugly.

Eight months later, Brandon died and it was one of the saddest days of my life. While I was not personally responsible for his health (which was a major problem in our relationship), I knew that his broken heart did not help and I am truly sorry it came to that conclusion.

After about six months of being single, I realized that the single life was not good for me.

BRIAN AND A RELOCATION

Because of my giving nature, I feel I am a better person inside of a committed relationship. Enter Brian. Brian was a blast from the past who was back in my hometown of Houston, Texas. After dating long distance for a few months, Brian asked me to return to Houston so we could work on our relationship and get married within the year. I agreed. I transferred with my job, packed up my furniture and my 16-year-old daughter and we moved back to Houston. Another drastic step for love.

The day I arrived in Houston, Brian picked me up from the airport. As we were driving, he looks me dead in my eyes and says, "Why are you here?" "Excuse me," I replied. "What do you mean, why am I here?" I said. "I'm here because of all of the plans we made. We are getting married, remember?" He turned away from me and said quietly, "Yeah! I remember." I thought to myself, what the heck is going on? After dropping me off at my mother's home, Brian disappeared for a week. I couldn't find him. He wouldn't answer my calls. When I went by his house, he wouldn't answer the door. Needless to say, I had been dumped.

One thing I will not do is beg for someone to love me. He should be glad that I am not a different kind of woman, because I surely thought about busting the windows out of his car, keying it and slashing his tires. He really should be glad. My heart was broken, but I kept on stepping.

KISSING SOME FROGS: JOHN, ANTHONY, THEN ROBERT

I kissed a lot of frogs on my journey back to marriage; I had relationships with John, the verbal abuser, and Anthony, the liar and cheater, and then came Robert.

Robert was not really my type. He was 16 years older than me and very charming. He was the first man that ever bought me a gift without me asking. He was the first one to reach into his pocket and hand me money. He was the first one to pay for everything when we were dating. He was a take-charge man and as an independent, "I got this" woman, I appreciated a man who could take charge and handle things. It was really sexy and I grew to like him, a lot.

One month into our relationship, Robert tells me that he had prostate cancer in recent years. He had his prostate removed and he couldn't get an erection. Huh? At 43 years old, what was I supposed to do with that information. He already had a consultation scheduled with a urologist to receive a penal implant which he did two months into our relationship. I swear I have been through the gamut of relationships. Now, I've fallen in love with a man who has to have a penal implant. What next? What was next showed up a month later, three months into our relationship.

From the beginning of our relationship, Robert complained about a pain in his side and he had an unusual amount of gas. I thought, he sure does fart a lot and we barely know each other. I began to ask questions. "What does the pain feel like? Have you been to a specialist?" It turns out, as a typical man, he had not been to the doctor and was self-medicating for what he thought might be an ulcer with antacids. Me, being the take charge one said, "Let me get you to a specialist." I remember it like it was yesterday.

Robert had his first colonoscopy at 59 years old and the doctor said, "I'm sorry to tell you that you have a tumour in your intestines and it looks like colon cancer." It felt like I had been punched in the gut. "You have to have emergency surgery because your colon is about to rupture and you will die without it." Within a week, we were in the hospital again; the second time in three months. By this time, I had fallen for him and because I knew he needed me to care for him, I decided to stay. Although the surgery was successful, it left him with a colostomy bag. What? So now, my man has a bionic penis and he craps in a bag through a hole in his stomach. I must really be in love! Two months later I did what any other vibrant, successful, young woman would do, I married him. Another drastic step. On some level, I subconsciously thought I was making up for not being there for Brandon.

Robert and I got married six months after meeting, on a Saturday, in a beautiful garden. Four days later Robert had his first chemo session. I joked that our honeymoon was at the cancer hospital. This started our two-and-a-half-year cancer war. To say it was hard would be putting it mildly. As you can imagine, Robert was angry and hurt that he was dying. He would say to me, that he was sorry that he met me so late in life and that he couldn't be the person he wanted to be for me. Even though we were fighting his cancer, we did manage to take six trips in the short time we were married and those times were great. We laughed a lot.

Make no mistake about it, this was absolutely the hardest time in my life. Besides watching someone you love die, I was in school getting my Bachelor's degree, working full-time and being a caregiver.

On November 1, 2012, Robert passed away at the hospice where we were married (we both loved their garden) surrounded by his family and friends, laughing and talking about the good times they brought him. Robert taught me that I have it in me to be a caregiver and to love someone else unconditionally. I will always be grateful for the love he showed me and the great times we shared.

SINGLE AGAIN AND THEN CAME WALTER

Now, I'm single yet AGAIN! Of course, I'm not immediately setting my sights on another relationship, but I think it is always in the back of my mind. Eight months later, in comes Walter. Walter was a guest on my Internet radio show and he was an aspiring speaker. He had an amazingly sexy voice and I was captivated just to hear him talk. He connected with me after the interview and we formed a friendship. Walter was safe because he lived in Milwaukee and I lived in Houston. We started out video chatting over Skype, discussing business, and I was coaching him.

The attraction grew and we began to have a real connection. Walter was divorced and wanted a relationship, just not with me. Whenever we would spend time together it was electric. We had an amazing chemistry. He would always say I was his best friend and excellent wife material.

He spoke out of both sides of his mouth. He would say he loved me, then he would say he didn't see a future with me. After a year and a half, Walter broke off his friendship with me (he would never admit there was a relationship), citing that he just didn't love me the way I loved him. My heart was broken and I was devastated! I thought what we had was almost perfect. When we broke up, I didn't show any emotion. I didn't scream, cry, curse or anything. I just said, okay. I figured this was another man that I would just get over in time, but this time was different.

SINGLE AND ILLNESS

About eight days later, I woke up with a stomach ache. I thought it was gas, and it would pass. When the pain didn't pass, I went to the hospital. It turns out that I had a hernia in my intestines and they had to do emergency surgery. Long story short, I became septic and was in a coma for ten days.

My life was on the line and the doctors weren't optimistic about my full recovery. After much prayer and medical care, I have made a full recovery and am a living testimony to God's grace. The lesson I learned is not to hold in emotion. While I don't believe that the breakup caused my body to breakdown, I do believe that holding in my grief and anger was the catalyst to trigger the pain.

After my illness, I resolved to be happy and content in my singleness. My business was flourishing and

I was traveling all over the country speaking. I fully recovered from my illness and I was happy with myself. Apparently, God knew what I needed and had other plans for my life.

MAY BE GARY IS THE ONE!

Approximately a year after my breakup with Walter, I met Gary. We were introduced by mutual friends. After speaking on the phone to Gary for ten minutes he said, "I'm looking for a wife." I thought, that's direct and unusual. "Well, I'm not looking for a husband," I said. I really had become content in my singleness. I immediately got into business mode. I said to him, "Let's keep talking, I'll listen to hear what you're looking for and I'll see who I can refer you to." He kept talking. By the end of that first conversation, I said to him, "You really are a nice man." hope you find what you're looking for, and in the meantime, if I think of someone nice for you, I will introduce you.

That was my, "Don't call me, I'll call you close. It didn't work. He called me the next day, and the next and the next. We met in person shortly after and the rest, as they say, is history. Gary too was a very nice man. He was charming. He had a southern accent that was cute and he had a bad boy side that I kind of liked. Gary sent me virtual flowers and poems every day. I really loved the attention. A month and a half after we met, he asked me to marry him and I said, "Yes." Gary and I met and were married within five months. Another drastic step. Today, we are very happy and in love. I'm grateful that he too was a drastic stepper and set his past relationships to the side to allow me to love him.

Looking back on the love stories of my life, I admit I've had some great ones. They haven't been easy and I've had my heart broken more than I care to admit. But I can't help it, I love; everything about being in love. Living in love and thriving in love. I guess I'm a hopeless romantic. I have made lots of mistakes. Chose the wrong man. Gave too much. Got cheated on and got used, but through it all, I still love *"**Love Unboxed**"*.

My advice to you is to love drastically. It may not turn out perfectly but if you love from your heart, your love will be returned. I've never been afraid to love even after divorce, death, and heartbreak. Remember, you can't win if you don't take the drastic step to trust and love again.

Will this be the last chapter on my relationship?

ABOUT THE AUTHOR

Toni Harris Taylor is a motivational and marketing speaker who helps people to take drastic steps to achieve success. Toni's life story includes amazing drastic steps for love. She has survived the terrible

D's of relationships — divorce, debilitating illness, death, doubt and disappointment. Somehow, she manages to pick herself up and keep on stepping even when she could not see what was ahead of her. Toni's story is one of rebound after life's curve balls that has led her to be in a loving, thriving happy marriage. In her story, you will experience the triumphs, heartbreaks and the recovery that lets you know, if she can keep stepping, you can too.

CONTACT:

http://www.toniharristaylor.com/
Toni@ToniHarrisTaylor.com

PART FOUR

ABUSE, PAIN, FEAR AND FREEDOM

THE ANSWER LIES WITHIN US
Evakarin Wallin: Sweden

"Life is full of beauty. Notice it. Notice the bumble bee, the small child, and the smiling faces. Smell the rain, and feel the wind. Live your life to the fullest potential, and fight for your dreams."

~ Ashley Smith

It was our second date. The anticipation was conversely making me both happy and nervous at the same time. It was early springtime and the sun was shining through the bare trees waiting for their new leaves. The air was chilly, but I felt warm. We had known each other for three years being nothing more than friends. He was married while I was in a relationship. I always enjoyed his company; I thought he was a nice person. During the period of our friendship his marriage ended in divorce and I broke up my relationship.

On our first date my expectation was just to have something to drink, good conversation, just an enjoyable evening. We laughed a lot and both had a really good time. We realized that we had many common interests and values. Suddenly I could feel the energy between us change and our relationship turned into something else. I would never have thought that he would be interested in me. And I had not seen him as a potential partner before either.

It felt fresh and new, these were not what I had planned for myself. After my last breakup, I had decided that it would be just me and my children. I was fed up with men and lousy relationships. My relationships up until then had not been as supportive as I would have liked them to be. I always had an underlying feeling that my partners and I were not wanting the best for each other. I could not understand why.

Suddenly everything blurred as my relationship history began flashing in front of my eyes. My feet lost touch of the ground. I felt like I was hanging from a wall, holding on just by my fingertips. The ground had vanished. I was about to do something bad. I did not know what, but the purpose was to destroy this relationship. I was not worthy of a man like this. I felt dirty and he was so pure. It would end it before it even began. I could not help myself.

When I think back to the early eighties, I remember it as a fun time. I was out partying and had a lot of friends. But somehow, I ruined that for myself. I did not see it coming. Looking back in time I can now see that I had a subconscious belief about myself. It would say, "I was not worthy of having that much fun." I also had low self-esteem and that made me destroy the good things I had. If you would have asked me about that then, I would have denied it because I was totally unaware of it.

The evening I met the future father of my first daughter, I was at a night club sitting with some friends talking away. I turned my head around, met his eyes just before he disappeared behind a pillar. In that moment, which lasted less than a second I knew he would come and ask me to dance. And he did.

He was very handsome, dark hair and slightly brown skin. When I found out that he came from

Iraq, it made him more interesting to me. It was an opportunity to get to learn about parts of the world I had only heard about. I have heard about the Orient. I was picturing the colours and fragrances, imagining the jingling sound of jewellery from the belly dancers.

He had escaped from the war between Iran and Iraq, migrating to France, but actually ending up in Sweden. He did not want to fight in a war. I honoured that and believed him to be a very kind and warm person, and in the beginning of our relationship, that is exactly how he was.

Within a few months, he moved in with me. It was then that things started to change for the worse bit by bit. He suddenly would get angry for no apparent reason. I felt bad wondering what I did wrong. Thinking I would try better next time, but the more I tried the worse it became. It was like living with Dr Jekyll and Mr. Hyde. Sometimes he was warm and kind, then without reason he was furious and aggressive. He escaped one war, but was now starting another.

By the time, I realized that I could not go on like this anymore, we had started a business together and were expecting our first child. During this time, I had cut all the cords to my friends. I think I did it because I was ashamed over my situation. I wanted to keep up the façade. I felt totally alone and did not know what to do or where to go. I was stuck.

We had come into a vicious circle. If I did something (or did not do something) he got angry. I became sad, crying and feeling sorry for myself. Then I got grumpy. When I was grumpy, he was the kindest and when I came around and back to a balance, it did not take long before we started all over again.

The love was over and it was all about surviving. I remember thinking, "Why is it so difficult to live together in peace? Why can we not just be friendly with each other?"

I was dreaming of a different kind of relationship, where two best friends and lovers that wanted the best for each other.

I believe that I attracted him because of my low self-esteem. He wanted a woman that he could dominate. He pushed me down even more and more, until I was so small that I would die if it continued. There was no option. I had my baby girl. I could not leave her. I was visioning her future to be bright. I wanted her to be happy. How could I guide her to that when I was not happy and my relationship with her father was one of war. I had to change my situation, but how?

THE MIRACLE

I guess I was praying for a miracle without knowing what I was doing. One day it came in a form of a movie on the TV. It was a film starring Shirley MacLaine called "Out on a Limb."

My partner and I were watching it together. I was judging the film. The movie is about her spiritual awakening. It inspired many people around the world to start their own journey. Those Hollywood divas can say and do anything I thought to myself.

Suddenly I heard him say, "This is almost like what the Koran says." What did he just say? How could something coming from two so different worlds sound almost the same. In that sentence, what he said totally changed my attitude. I became interested and wanted to know more. I found books to read. I learned about "affirmations" and that you have the ability to change your reality.

I got hooked to my new mission, although I was sceptical about the idea that it could be so easy to change a life just by changing thoughts. It sounded too simple. If it worked that way, why did not everybody already do that? One part of me believed in the concept and another part doubted it. The ideas went back and forth in my mind. If this was true, I did not want to miss out, so I continued on my path of personal development and spiritual awakening.

I had one big concern, that if I created my reality and everything around me was a mirror showing me myself, then how had I fallen into a relationship with someone that was so mean to me when I was so kind and caring?

I needed help to understand why. It took a long time for me to get it. When I finally was able to receive the answer, it was the last thing I wanted to hear.

What the universe was telling me was that I had to set boundaries, learn to say no, to stand up for myself. At that point, I did not know what I wanted so it was difficult to create a vision of any kind. I could only be in the moment ask myself, "Is this what I want from life?"

It did give me strength. I slowly started to stand up for myself. I learned to say "No." That made him even more angry. He thought I was evil, but now I was stronger inside and the more I grew, the weaker his ability was to dominate me.

Most of all, I wanted to keep the family together. The stronger I got, the more I could see the possibility for us to stay together. I felt better inside and it seemed to me that the fighting was becoming less and less. If you go from bad to better, you can handle change.

Then, one day he started shouting at me again, and without thinking, I just took my two-year old daughter in my arms said goodbye. I walked out of the front door.

This was just a few weeks before I was about to give birth to our second child. He did not expect me to leave and neither did I. It just happened in the moment. I understood that finally I had become strong enough to choose me.

I went to a friend of mine and asked if I could sleep on her sofa until I got myself a place to live. Two weeks later I moved into my new apartment. I was free. I was leaving five years of mental and emotional struggle behind me. I could not have been happier.

WHEN YOU LEAVE A BAD RELATIONSHIP, YOU TAKE HALF OF IT WITH YOU

What I learned over the coming years was that if you leave a bad relationship you take half of it with you. I had grown and learned a lot, but there was still so much left for me to understand.

Thirteen years later, I was there on my second date, hanging on by my fingertips. It was possibly the beginning of a new relationship. Could I do it or should I let go and fall? I still had a lot of limiting beliefs about myself. It was those limiting beliefs that were pushing me to do something to destroy this relationship before it started so we could return to just being friends. I was fighting with myself.

If you ever been standing on a cliff, and felt the urge to jump then this was just how I was feeling. I did not want to, but something inside me told me it was for the best.

I saw my life being acted out like a movie in my head. I could see myself from a distance and all the wrong paths I had taken. How I had acted in relationship to my partners. Suddenly, I could see why I never felt enough and why I never had a lasting loving relationship.

I could feel the ground under my feet again. My vision got clear again and I saw that we were still sitting together having a coffee. I realized this small thing was okay. The man in front of me was patient, strong and loving. He saw something in me that I had not seen in myself. "You are an unpolished diamond", he said. My life was about to take on a new route.

THE PRESENT DAY

Today, I can look back at my life and can connect the dots. I am very happy to be where I am. My beautiful children are happy in their lives and I am so grateful for that. During the years when they were growing up, my life was very stressful in many ways. That has reflected in them as well.

I am so grateful that I never gave up, that I had my vision of my children being happy and that I understood the way even though I did not know how at the time. I am also grateful for my new husband who came into our lives at a time when they could see him as a healthy role model. Almost another thirteen years has now passed since our second date and it still feels fresh. This is the relationship I was longing for back in the days when I got a dose of anger almost every day.

I see now that this was the relationship that had been waiting for me all along. I was just not just aware of it. It was like he was planted for me as a gift from life. I just had to follow my path and there he would be.

At our wedding, my son read a poem in which to me describes the respectful and loving relationship we still have.

ON MARRIAGE

You were born together, and together you shall be forevermore. You shall be together when the white wings of death scatter your days. Ay, you shall be together even in the silent memory of God. But let there be spaces in your togetherness, and let the winds of the heavens dance between you.

Love one another, but make not a bond of love: Let it rather be a moving sea between the shores of your souls. Fill each other's cup but drink not from one cup.

Give one another of your bread but eat not from the same loaf. Sing and dance together and be joyous, but let each one of you be alone, even as the strings of a lute are alone though they quiver with the same music.

Give your hearts, but not into each other's keeping. For only the hand of Life can contain your hearts. And stand together yet not too near together: For the pillars of the temple stand apart, and the oak tree and the cypress grow not in each other's shadow.

- Kahlil Gibran

ABOUT THE AUTHOR

Evakarin Wallin is a mindset coach, speaker, author and founder of Freedom Based Mindset, a technique that changes limitations into possibilities. She is in the forefront of how to use the subconscious mind to reprogram limiting beliefs into empowering beliefs that allow you to manifest easily and effortlessly.

In Sweden, she was one of the first life coaches which meant that nobody knew what life coaching was when she started out. And she did not know how to sell. So, she hired her own coach and learned the basics of sales and marketing.

Very soon she realized many small business owners needed to learn marketing, so she became a marketing coach. She did that for several years but could not break through to the next level in her own business. It was like hitting the glass ceiling.

Then she started to investigate what was going on within her. That was the start of a journey that took four years and led to Freedom Based Mindset, a technique that literally releases fears and limitations instantly.

She is the author of *Boost Your Business With A Book* and has had several of her articles published in Ascala Magazine and More Business Magazine.

CONTACT:

Website: http://evakarinwallin.se
Facebook: https://www.facebook.com/evakarin.wallin
LinkedIn: http://www.linkedin.com/in/evakarinwallin

HOW I MET MY HUSBAND
Laura Buxó: Spain

"We think sometimes that poverty is only being hungry, naked and homeless. The poverty of being unwanted, unloved and uncared for is the greatest poverty. We must start in our own homes to remedy this kind of poverty."

~ Mother Teresa

I will never forget the 30th April 2011. It is a day etched in my memory. My friend Laila lives in Egypt and this was the day I received her text instructing me to introduce myself to an Egyptian boy, who was and still is a tour guide. She did not hide her intentions as she tried to persuade me to send him a friend request through social media.

Laila had a plan to get me married, which was the exact opposite of my intentions. Her choice did not inspire me either especially since my last cheating, lying boyfriend had been an Egyptian tour guide as well, I was not going to make that mistake again. It is a job that men with the gift to chat up woman like to do so they can meet lots more women and sleep with them!

It had been a terrible 4 years' experience of being told it was my imagination and really, I still do not know how, but one day, I just woke up and said "it is over." Good for me, maybe I wasted too much time or maybe it was the time I just needed to feel strong enough just to do it. Anyway, just because this story was still fresh and raw inside me, hurting so much and because the boy was also Egyptian and working as a tour guide, I refused her request.

My friend, as a good Egyptian, continued. She said, "This boy was different. He was a faithful guy." She lied saying further, down playing that she wanted me to contact him just to have a friend in Egypt. So, I am still asking myself why I send this friend request: because I really believe I would win a new friend? Or maybe, I was trying to find someone to love me? I sent the friend request. After one or maybe two minutes, he accepted my friend request...yeah! It seemed like he was waiting for me. Immediately by return, he wrote me a private message introducing himself. He was well educated. He was different. He did not give me any idea that he was interested in a "love" relationship. In Europe, it is normal that boys and girls can just be friends, but that is not my experience in Egypt, especially with men that work in the tourism industry. It is normal that in the first conversation that you are the most wonderful woman they have ever met, their soul mate, saying "You are so beautiful! Will you marry me?" So, that was a great bonus for him in my book. He seemed a normal boy. Great! I made him wait a whole day before I give him a reply to his message, and that was our beginning.

Over the first week, we sent one message every day, trying to know a little bit more about each other. I discovered that my friend had lied to me, of course! I called her wanting know why she lied to me. Her response was so true, "Because you would say no, but now you are trying to get to know him. It is safe.

Everything is over the Net, so you do not have any obligation! So just enjoy this experience." I do admit it was so easy talking to Farouk. I started becoming glued to my phone, constantly checking for messages, just waiting for his daily message. It told me it was the same for him. It was amazing, every time I got one message I felt happy, lovely, strong, and we were just talking about our lives!! In the second week, we started to send two messages per day, one in the morning and the second at night. Every time it was more and more amazing. It was so exciting. We started to talk about our past relationships and how much pain we felt. He was falling in love with a Spanish girl and I was with an Egyptian boy. Wow, what else? We could understand each other perfectly. Both of us love ancient Egyptian history, but in that moment, we were sad because of the Egyptian revolution that started in January 2011. It meant no work for him and of course, a lot of pain to Egyptian people.

After a few days, the texts became phone calls every day. Our connection was amazing. Two months later, we met each other face to face in Cairo and in that moment, we started our "love" relationship. I was completely in love with him, but my intuition was telling me that he did not feel the same way. I decided to ignore this feeling and just continued our story.

He was not completely perfect in my eyes, I did not like his impatience and would manifest itself when he called me. I had to answer quickly. If not, there was always a question. "Where were you?" or "What are, you doing?" or "Why you do not answer me?"

He was not interested in my responses. Like everyone, I had a life outside my phone. The answers were very easy, "work, toilet, did not hear, the battery was flat." He made me feel scared that if I had not answered in the moment I would risk losing him. So, I gave him permission to control me at any time, in every moment, everywhere, so began my toxic relationship.

MY ENGAGEMENT AND MY MARRIAGE.

I remember one day I was so angry with my mum. We were still boyfriend and girlfriend, with Farouk living in Cairo and me living in Barcelona. Farouk had asked me to travel to Madrid that weekend as a change to our normal habit and he planned us being away some days. In Madrid, I had some friends more than friends, Almudena and Francisco we more like my second parents. We were going to s with them. I arrived first and would wait for Far

In the morning, I talked with Farouk with a Fac call. He was still in Cairo. I found him very n and I just did not know why. After the call feeling guilty without any reason, but the talked to me left me with that feeling. I wer lunch with my friends, being joined by so friends from Costa Rica. They took me to a very nice place in Madrid. It was a small, but very comfortable restaurant.

Something was strange. They also looked nervous. I was sure that Farouk was not going to appear as planned because I saw him on facetime and he was in Cairo. It was not a possibility but something was about to happened. I was sure about that.

After eating, we went to drink coffee in a very romantic place. It was a terrace in front of Madrid's Cathedral. The views were spectacular. I was beginning to feel a little bit angry because everyone was acting very strange. I knew they were lying to me and I did not like that. I am very good at seeing n someone is lying to me. Almudena received ne call. It was Farouk. She put the hands free all of us begun to talk to him. When Farouk me, everyone went silent. All of them were ne, I just did not know what to do or say. re my love?" he asked. "Yes," I could "Listen my love, I want to ask you a ry important that is why I want our e with you. I would prefer to do anyway…would you marry me?" ne with the loveliest flowers I

)ck. A lot of questions came ue?" "Am I really engaged?"

I phoned him. I needed to talk to him. I needed to realise this was true. He was still nervous and he talked to me in a very bad way saying that a friend was waiting for him and he was late. He ended the call as he had no time to talk to me. My friends were so happy yet I was feeling sad. Not because of the "rushed" proposal, but because he had no time to talk to me afterwards.

We walked with my amazing flowers and all the old women we met on the street were wishing me good luck. My friends and I took pictures, to capture this moment of my love and happiness. I was checking my phone, but no news from Farouk. I was still in shock.

At night, I sent him all the pictures and we Facetime called. I needed to ask him some questions. "So, honey, are you happy? Did you like the proposal? I was nervous all morning. I would love to be there next to you. Did they give you the flowers I sent to you? Did you like the flowers?"

"Oh yes of course, I really loved them. It was a pity that you were not here, but thank you very much for this proposal. I must tell you that I am still in shock. I could not imagine that you want to get married. We have never talked about this before, but I am happy you did it."

"Honey, sorry I was with my friend Hassan all evening. We had dinner together then watched a football match on TV. Egypt played this evening and we won the match. So now, I tell you good night. I am so happy you like the proposal and you have accepted it. You must know it is not a good idea to share it on social networks because with these pictures someone could give us the evil eye, so please remove them now. Even do not say we are engaged. We do not want any bad luck at all. I cannot talk more tonight, there is a football show on television now that I really want to watch. Do what I have told you right now and do not post anything about our engagement again. Sweet dreams."

My mouth was still open. What was going on? It was a dream or a nightmare? Again, he had not time to talk to me and I could not share my pictures or happiness in any of my social networks. Evil's eye? Really? So, I removed all the pictures and love status. My phone rang almost immediately. It was Farouk. "Are you stupid? Thank God you removed the pictures, but you do not have to say you are single. You are engaged. Change it right now, but do not say my name. Do you get it now?" and he rang off without letting me say a word.

MARRIED

That was the first time he had ever shouted at me. Giving orders, angry, with violence in his words. The saddest thing is I believed all the words he was telling me and I did all the things he was telling me to do. In that moment, I found these things normal, I really believed that it all was my fault. You may ask me why, but I think it is because I had no self-esteem. When I was a teenager, I was bulled twice. The first one when I was 14 and the second one when I was 16. I learned how to hate myself. I thought that good things only happened to others and I only deserved the worst. I accept that my fiancé would find fault in me and would not be kind, it was the price I must pay as the man wanted to marry me. It was June 2013 when we married in Spain and start a life there together. It was also the start of a war between us. Everything had to be done in the Egyptian tradition; food, time of breakfast, lunch and dinner. I had to forget about going to the beach, wearing a bikini, about makeup and of course, forget about wearing tops or any type of clothes that can show any part of my body in a way that in his opinion was at all "sexy".

No perfume either as it might attract men to me. If I wanted to see a friend, I needed permission and he would always phone me while I was with my friends, saying, "Do you forget me? At what time are you going to come back? What are you doing all this time?" His constant need to be with me left me feeling guilty for being with a friend and not with him. I stopped enjoying being with my friends as I felt like I was deliberately hurting him by going out.

Our sex life was even worse, it died shortly after we married, and well, if you asked him, it was because of me. He is insisted that I was always ready for him. That would mean to be completely shaved, even my arms. I must wear sexy clothes and perfume around the house, but only for him. Never outside or inside if we had guests.

It is normal to want to be ready and sexy for our partner, but if your partner ordered you to do it then things change. If my arms were not exactly as he demanded, and believe me, I have no hair in my arms naturally, I would have to shave them and he did not like waiting, he got very angry, so he would just leave me alone. The moment would be lost.

He would blame me, saying I was not ready for him, and that I was a dirty woman who was not taking care of herself. I could not tell you the actual words he would use because they cannot be printed. One time, he told me "You must be like a bitch at home for me, put make up, sexy clothes, perfume, etc. Do you think I find you sexy with your pyjamas on?"

I began having anxiety attacks daily. I was feeling like the worst woman and wife in all the god forsaken world. But something inside me was making me stop doing what he was asking me to do. At last, a little bit of common sense. I stopped doing what he asked me to do for sex as I did not want to be touch by him at all. I knew he was not good for me, but I needed more time as my low self-esteem was effecting my judgment. The anxiety was growing and growing every day. He knew how to press the button to activate these anxiety attacks and he did it every time for the next three years.

One night, I woke and could not breathe. I begged him to take me to hospital. The doctor was fantastic. He diagnosed my anxiety and arranged for me to see a psychologist. Without them I would be lost. I thank God for letting them into my life to help me, especially the doctor as he continued to help me even after his referral.

DIVORCE

I decided to get divorced in August 2016. We were living in Egypt and I did not know how to tell him. I knew I wanted to be alone, without him. It was very scared about living alone. I talked to my psychologist about it. It took me until December 2016 to tell Farouk.

WHAT I HAVE LEARNED FROM THIS

Everything that happens has a reason, of this I am sure. I needed to meet Farouk to understand that the only person who is going to take good care of me is MYSELF.

If you are unhappy and do not feel strong enough to break the cycle, then find help as I did.

I have learned that we do not pay enough attention to the signs that our inner voices tell us.

We must live this moment, here and now. If you do not like the situation you are in, leave it, you do not need it. Do not be scared of leaving. Leave everything that hurts you. If you have questions, look inside yourself and I swear, you will find all the answers to questions. Scared? I prefer to call it being awesome! Do not allow anyone to treat you in a way that you do not feel comfortable. But do not forget to treat yourself right first, if you do not respect yourself why should anyone else? Do not be scared of loving someone again. Give always all your love, but never expect someone to love you. You are awesome so love yourself! And if this person cannot see it, it's his or her problem, it is not yours.

Today I am happy. My life is full of joy because I realise that life full of new opportunity. I am alive, healthy and have faith that I will meet the man of my dreams one day. Real love exists, I do not have any doubt and the best is about to come.

ABOUT THE AUTHOR

Laura Buxó, born 25th January 1980 in Spain. She studied Business Studies, she is a Finance

Director and owns a travel agency in her home town Sabadell. Laura suffered a period of intense bullying in school, which affected her self-esteem. In 2013, she married an Egyptian. It should have been her perfect love story, but in reality, he inflicted systematic psychological abuse. It took her three years to escape and is now divorcing him. She is an expert in body language. According to Laura, it is amazing what people say without talking!

Her story will touch your heart.

CONTACT

writetolaurabuxo@outlook.com

MELANCHOLY LOVE
Gloria Boma Alabo: Nigeria

"A wise woman wishes to be no one's enemy; a wise woman refuses to be anyone's victim."

~ Maya Angelou

The man saw himself as the Lion in my life and that it was in his power to hold me in the palm of his hand. I gave him that Lion status. Everyone has a limit and he pushed mine. Now he cannot look me in the face in case he sees my eyes. Today, it is he that bows while I walk head high. By God's grace, I have regained my self-esteem, respect and worthiness as a woman.

I do not encourage women to go through pain to make them realize the reason for living. It is better to read other women's stories and learn from them. My fellow women, you will wonder why, as my story unfolds in the words that follow, why I was prepared to endure so much. Do not hold me to blackmail or ridicule me for my decisions, instead wonder about my life as I unroll the years I spent with Musa and be refreshed in your own life. Do not shed a tear, but smile like I smile with every day God gives me!

The freedom of being free from cruelty and assault is the priceless gift that God has now given to me, but this was not always so. I had to earn it. I celebrate God in my life. He is the pilot of my affairs.

I am not dating, but have a few good mature friends with whom I relate closely. As for men, well, let it be clear, *I am in charge,* so do not exploit me. Laugh laugh laugh "Waooooo", life is beautiful.

GROWING UP

My late father, Mr Edward N.D Alabo, was told a story by his grandma, Mama Sella, that if a man fathers a girl, then that family will always grow and become a strong family. My daddy grew up with that superstitious belief. He even kept a native wrapper for thirty years given to him by his mother, Racheal Iwo.

I was a child born through "love" and occupied a special place in my family's heart, especially in my father's. The love bond between us was great and I believed no man could live up to my dad.

APPREHENSIVE RELATIONSHIP

I was greatly apprehensive about getting married. Wife abuse was the norm in my society with little protection for women. I did not want it to be my life story.

As a young Christian lady, this fear was debated in 1990, during a marriage seminar organized by the Nigerian Fellowship of Evangelical students (NIFES), of which I was member. It was during one of these National Conferences, back in August 1991, held in Owerri Imo State, that I met Musa Kabirua. He was a student from the northern part of my country, Nigeria.

This was the man I would marry some years later. We began writing to each other immediately and, in December 1991, he proposed marriage. I accepted in July 1993. I was twenty-one.

He was still studying, and we recognised that until he finished it was not practical to marry, so I promised to wait, but this was not without its challenges. I decided to relocate back to the North, his home town. My father consented because I was familiar with the area having finished my National Youth Service there. Crazy I guess, but I was in love. He was my first and true love. When you are young, you make sacrifices to be happy. We were both Christians, so before we married I lived with a friend. I knew it was risky and impulsive to move especially with no assurance of a job, but I needed to be near him.

The day came in May 1994 when I left the shore of Port Harcourt and moved the 970 kilometres north (Equivalent of 7 days of cycling). I had only been away two months, when I received the very sad news that my protector and darling father had died.

MARRIAGE AND FAMILY LIFE

I blessed God, who helped me find a teaching job in a tertiary institution in October 1995. My relationship, however, stagnated, so we separated in 1996. Thirteen months later, we reconciled, but broke up again for three months. Eventually, we did reconcile. In all that time, I never guessed or suspected his reckless attitude towards women as we resided in different states.

Our turbulent courtship had lasted over five years. We had to wait for him to finish his studies. I was delighted when he was retained to work with NIFES as a student pastor. Deep smile!! I made up my mind, we would marry six months later in November 1998. "Waoooo", how thrilled and happy was I!!

I had married my love, passion, and treasure. My pet name for him was "Trel". I really loved his manners and I accorded him with so much love and respect. The first time we made love, it was not easy or exciting, but we adjusted after I prayed about it. "Oooooh", sex was really great (*Kissed my fingers: I laugh, please do not mind Me!*).

In February 1999, I was pregnant!! The thought of motherhood was exciting, not excluding the stress associated with it. Four months in and I became depressed, feeling I was struggling alone without any sense of responsibility coming from my husband.

I wanted to resign my job and relocate to Ilorin, Kwara State. Blessed be God, I did not, but waited. It would have been devastating for me given the event that was about to happen, which unknown to me turned out to be the start of the story of my life! As my due date approached, I did apply for my maternity, leaving for Ilorin in August 1999.

In September, I discovered unusual behaviour from my husband towards a Sister Corp called Monica, who was serving with the ministry (NIFES) in Ilorin. My husband, who has never bought a gift in his life, I found out used my money to buy a lady's hand bag for this woman. When I found out, it deeply upset me. When I expressed my displeasure, he responded he did it, on behalf of the family. It did not make sense, as I was shouldering all the family demands, including my unborn baby. How did winning this woman's favour help us?

My due date was arriving, but on this fateful day, his mother and I, left for Sunday worship. My husband was already dressed, when we left, but never arrived in church! I was wondering why?

I found out that, he had gone to peep at Monica in her nudity while she was bathing. A student pastor! How ironic!

She saw him and in an attempt to chase him away with a bucket half filled with water, she banged her wrist on a slide window. She incurred a serious injury. The voyeur, realising in his act he had not been formally recognised, pretended to run into the apartment to help. Her screaming attracted the neighbours as she blead profusely, almost losing her life, requiring her to be admitted into a private hospital. It was the same one that I had registered for the delivery of my baby.

On reaching home after Sunday worship, I found he was not home. He arrived a few minutes later, looking stressed. "Monica is in danger!" She was injured by an unknown person and needed cash for the purchase of blood. He had taken the money I had saved for my baby and I to pay for Monica's care. The situation was pitiful and the news about the incident spread. The Brethren visited her, they prayed and cursed, and he was there, saying Amen for her.

I never knew my husband was such a great deceiver and womanizer. He was pastoring at the same time and ruining lives. In July 2000, Sister Monica forced him to confess his evil act against her. It was extremely difficult for me to believe, but it was true. He cried, I cried, and we ended up making love that night. I accepted the situation and decided to keep him. I lived with pain, betrayal and I burned inside with a great amount of uncertainty and distrust. My husband entered a period of sober reflection and repentance. It seemed genuine. "Ooooooo", was I absolutely wrong to have believed him.

Before Monica left Ilorin, I felt the need to plead for her forgiveness, so booked an appointment to meet her on 30/7/2000. I knelt before her crying, humiliated, ashamed and helpless. "Your husband says A and does Z." That was a big blow in my abdomen. I thought his repentance was genuine. I was to receive another one soon.

In August 2001, I was pregnant with our second baby. Considering my first delivery required a caesarean section, I registered with the teaching hospital knowing I needed a good gynaecologist. During one of my check-ups, I met another Sister Corp member with a calm look called Kate.

The very sight of her made me feel apprehensive. I doubted my husband's integrity as the pain was still lingering within me. It was barely three weeks to my delivery. Sister Kate, with an angry expression approached me. "Aunty, your husband just walked into my bathroom while I was bathing and held me." What! I was dazed. Not again. I could not believe what I just heard. This man wants to kill me!

He heard her complain while coming down the stairs. He had an evil smiley expression on his face. As my due date approached, I prayed, cried and praised God for favour that He would grant me a safe delivery. I could not deliver a 3.3kg baby the first time and this second was predicted a 4.2kg baby. I did not need him; I will deliver on my own. I checked into the hospital on the 14 May 2002, paid the bills as usual, praise to God for my mummy, who arrived just right on time supported by her cousin's sister's daughter, Minna.

Minna decided to stay and help with the baby in return for me sponsoring her education. I was grateful for the help, but then my husband started trying to mess with her in our home. I had to send her back home before the baby arrived. Finally, my baby born on the 16 May 2002. I was discharged ten days later.

Before I checked out, Kate visited me as she was about relocate back home. I ceased the moment to apologize and ask for her forgiveness as usual, but her response was, "your husband says A and does Z".

Two days on our return from the hospital my husband packed to leave for his elder sister's house in Lagos. He's done this on several occasions. My mummy's presence was a succour for me. Eventually, he put his resignation in and we relocated to my station in Kontagora. Sometimes I wondered if this was same man who held my hand and looked into my eyes with great expression of verbal and non-verbal expressions of love. Was it pretence that he could not tell me his real mind. The words, "I love you" were becoming more difficult to say, and occasionally, he will say, "you do not really know who I am my dear!" He was absolutely right! "Ooooo".

I battled over our finances. He started searching for a local job, which he secured, but quickly resigned from. He did this without any discussion. I had forgiven him three times, but I was not Superwoman. I loved my husband despite his infidelity towards me.

THE CRACKED WALL FELL

It was 31st July 2003 when he returned home having quit the little job he was doing in Lagos. We will manage, I told him. A few days later, at 3:00am he screamed loud. He had offensive blood coming out of his mouth. He was dying!

I started praying! I inserted my index and third finger into his mouth and suddenly his teeth closed tightly on my fingers. I struggled hard to pull out my fingers. I ran out of the apartment forgetting I was partly naked. I grabbed a wrapper and screamed for help. Colleagues came to my aid with medicines. He survived, but after that day I was scared to sleep. How could this man try to die on me!

In 2004, on returning home from work he asked me, "how can I say to you, welcome home? Why should I?"

"Aaaaah!" This was strange. I wave it off, but this was the start of something new. He started picking on every little thing from the pastor's sermon, to our neighbours, issues in our personal life, and worst of all, he started assaulting me verbally. On my part, I felt his aggressiveness was caused by his frustration from a lack of employment, so I took it upon myself to find him a post in my institution, no matter how small. For one year, I did that on a weekly basis, but I became pregnant again towards the end of 2004.

My husband had started bringing girls home in the name of fellowship. I observed he was a little reckless in defending them. His verbal assault now included name calling such as animals like rat, snake, cobra and other offensive words. On expressing my displeasure as I had not grown up in such an environment or home, occasionally he would apologize.

We relocated to another part of the campus at the end of 2004 and four months later I miscarried and lost the baby.

My husband had openly started dating a student named Nneka. "Waooo", I worked, and he spent the money on women. He crafted master lies, pretence and I was believing all the lies.

Gradually his reckless life began to expose him. In August 2005, he slept out and returned around 5:30am with the girl. I hit him on his chin and said, "you are destroying this home."

I received payback. He held my head and banged it on the floor three times. I was hurt and shocked. This was unbelievable! I still believed the whole reason for his behaviour was due to his lack of employment. I was on my knees again, pleading for God's forgiveness. His extramarital relationships were becoming more reckless. He had brought his lover to our matrimonial home without the slightest regard for me.

He despised me so much that I lost my worthiness as a wife to him. His lover, Nneka, gradually brought some belongings of hers to my home and I was warned that if I want peace, I dare not talk to her. If I did, it would be the beginning of problems for me. The intimacy between us dwindled. Even when I had desires or urges for sex, it was deliberately denied from me. Up to this day, I have not been told of the sin or offense I committed to deserve this treatment.

His heart has left and despite his cruelty to me, I still dearly love him and no sacrifice was too much for me and he exploited this to the maximum, knowing he was my weakness. With God's help, I began the process of securing a job for him as the opportunity came my way.

Finally, what I had prayed for happened. He had work. The expected had come into our hands. How excited I was, but unfortunately it became my woe. My pet name, "Pretty" was taken from me and passed to "somebody else".

In October 2005, he called me to the bedroom, a place I was no longer allowed to enter as I was restricted to the living room. He told me, "I want to be a free man. I have money and living my desired lifestyle. I am respected again. I no longer want the Bible in my life". On 17 October 2005, he told me point blank, "Just because I am married to you, does not mean you are part of my life. I will determine who stays in my life and who I stay with." It was only when I had money I seem to become his wife.

On 5th November 2005, he came home with his lover Nneka. I politely asked him to tell her to leave my home, it was my home and I went straight to the door, to open for her to leave. He locked the door and started beating me right in her presence. He held me by the neck, threw me into the bedroom with such force that I hit edge of the wooden bed. The damage inflicted by his throw still causes me agony today. The pain is still with me today, eleven years on. I require regular massage to help manage the physical injury inflicted on me by the man I love.

My woes were not over. We last had sex in September 2005, and would you believe it, I was pregnant again. I informed him of the outcome of the medical report, deep sigh!! It was like ----- I lacked words for it as I reflect over in my mind. The best I can describe is that I had an abominable thing in my belly that was like smelling sewage to him. He despised me so much. All he did was to ridicule and humiliated me as he desired.

"Waooooo waaaaa smiles", the ironic aspect was I was feeding him, his lover and paying the bills. He refused to take even the slightest responsibility. The quarrels and assaults increased and in April, he beat me while I was pregnant. I was on the edge of a nervous breakdown. As my pregnancy progressed, it became too difficult to drive so my husband had to start taxiing the boys. That became the end of my access to the family car, which I bought. He would sleep with the key in his pants and belt his trousers.

I lost every legitimate right as a wife. His lover, Nneka, would dictate his actions at home. I decided to return home to my family as it was best and safer for me. My unborn child and children would get love and support. I gave birth on the 19 July 2006 to my third son, a wonderful gift from God. I also now had informed my family of my plight and marital struggles.

You would not believe that this man actually came for the birth of his unborn child. He stayed only a day and left. He did not even "drop" a penny. As usual, I paid the whole bill like I had for my previous births, including food, transport and everything despite him earning good pay.

After the birth, I returned to my home. There was no food for my kids and the apartment was dirty. Nneka and my husband had left.

My agony had not yet reached its worst stage. Reader please do not relax. In October 2006, my husband returned with a new lady. Her name was Palmer. They arrived one evening to my home and said she will be staying here. What? Another woman again in my home; not this time.

A month later, I had dropped my boys with my neighbour's children for school. It was only across the road. As I walked back into my living room I met them having sex on my sofa.

Palmer and my husband were now installed full time in my home, smiles, "Hmmm Oooh God yeah". After 4 months, in February 2007, I insisted Palmer leave my home. I got the beating of my life and in self-defence, I took a plate and hit him on the head. It obviously must have hurt, he left me alone, but for one full week my bruising was so bad I could not face the natural light of the day. My friends came and wept for me, but I would not leave my home and the man I had made all these sacrifices for.

As I stayed away from work, he kept coming frequently to check on me, perhaps in the way a wild beast would checking its prey. I had to shoulder rumours of his behaviour spreading round the institution where we both work. This did not lead to peace for me as he started forcing himself on me in my vulnerable state. We "made love" at least twice in April of 2007. It had been eighteen months since our skin came close to each other. He knew his health status, but he never bothered about me. Two months later, a visit to the doctor confirmed by fears. The samples from my body taken the source of itching had been passed through a laboratory test. It was discovered I had urinary infection and was given medication. "Oooooo, my God." I knew I had become vulnerable to HIV/Aids as most of his sex pleasures were taken from the carriers of this disease.

I informed him and he was silent about it. I pleaded that if he insisted on having me, he should use a barrier as I wept over my life and the danger I knew that was coming. In the August and September 2007, he came again had sex with me without any protection. "My God", I froze my heart, panting, praying I would be safe. I got pregnant and had to abort since my previous childbirth processes had all been through caesarean section and this was expensive. In addition, he had passed me more infections. I contracted more sores and itching through his visits. I discovered after several visits to the doctors a virus known as genital warts. It is a reoccurring infection which I have treated for years and it has almost destroyed my vagina.

There is a saying used in my society that says, "crying relieves one of pain", but I do not find this true. It did not take my pain away. He mocked me time and time again. I cried and cried for almost two solid years. "Ooooo save me my God", I took a deep breath. What a life story I must tell.

It is now the 18 March 2008 and another 6 months have passed. My first son had become ill and was on medication. As the evening arrived, my husband's girlfriend, Palmer, was outside my apartment and my boys were outside playing. It was time for his medication and I called out for him through my bedroom window. There was no reply, so I called again. Musa instructed him not to come into the bedroom, so I took his medicine outside to him. I asked him to kneel as I administer it. On hearing my voice outside, Musa came to the window of his room and told him to stand up and to not disobey him. My son ignored him. My husband then raged immediately like a wild cat. He rushed out to try to attack me, but I made it to the living room before he managed to get there. I locked my door, petrified about the beating that was about to rain down on me. He started furiously banging the door forcing it open. I pushed back with all the strength I could summon, but it was not a greater power than his and the door started to open, I tried to push him away from coming at me.

"Ooooooh, my God", I thank you for the fact that I am still living today. I will never stop expressing my gratitude to God for saving me from death.

Musa began beating me. I could not take it this time, not again. I told him enough is enough. I took his clothes and threw them outside, saying he must leave my house. Our rages escalated, he started "Round 2" of his beating, which continued without a break until I succumbed and could not defend myself as I slipped into a state of unconsciousness. I was left there perhaps to die.

I regained consciousness. The taste of my blood on my lips. I was so close to death. It was clear this man had wanted to kill me just like that and would only tell lies as usual to hide the truth.

I walked crying through the two kilometres of streets to the Magistrate's Court. It was like I suddenly developed a partial insanity. I became reckless. I was losing my mind. It was difficult to breathe as my ribs and head were seriously affected, this was death coming. I had to report this man to the Magistrate. Who would protect me?

The security men at the Courts would not let me in. They told me to return home. I tried explaining I was too scared to return home and that if I did my husband would surely try to finish the job he had started. My husband arrived. My God, he lied to the guards saying that it was not him that had inflicted this beating, but it had been my mum. He shouted that it was my mother who was the one behind the whole problem.

We reported to Magistrate Court 11 the next day as instructed, but this came to nothing as it was public holiday. We could not see the judge until the 21 March. Finally, we had our hearing at the end of the day. I had not eaten after two days of waiting. The Magistrates Court was an informal setting of which my husband had experience. He knew the process giving him a big advantage over me, as was his eloquence. I was in a damaged body. My face was broken and all I seemed to be able to do was cry cry cry. I was starving, hungry too. I felt helpless and injured.

I believe in God. I believe that say your prayers and your wishes shall be granted. Honestly, I need to understand what that means. I complained of his frequent assaults and told of the women he keeps in our home. The judge insisted his latest woman be summoned so she could be told to leave. To my shock, my husband opted instead to choose her over me and to move out with her. I cried, held him, saying, "you are leaving me after all I had gone through in life just for your sexual pleasure?"

"Ooooooh ooooo!", he chose her and left his wife and children. I could not believe it. I am his wife. Was I alive? Is it reality or fiction that I am experiencing? It happened, "Oooo", my marriage was over.

He won and I was ruined (tears almost gathered in my eyes as I tell you his, but I try to cover with a smile). All my romantic dreams about love, marriage, home was shattered before me. "Oh God, why me?" I ask. I never ceased asking for some good months. Just a little bit of happiness, please. I came out of the marriage injured, depressed, battered, cheated, infected with genital warts, high blood pressure, no self-esteem, no dignity, ashamed and no self-respect. I thought, I cannot live without him. I was so attached emotionally to him. I wept and wept. They were the tears of my soul.

THE SUN WILL ALWAYS RISE TOMORROW

My tears continued for a more few years, but gradually they began to reduce. I fell ill on 17 April 2008, the eve of my 40th birthday. I visited the doctor. After reading a blood pressure of 175/115, he said madam you are carrying your past stresses with you. It is better to look at what you have going forward. You have your life to live and children to take care off. Please, accept the good things. He was a good doctor. He was the one that had properly diagnosed genital warts. Without him I probably would have died within two weeks.

Honestly, it was pretty difficult during the initial separation period especially when the one you love dearly rejects you completely. He met another lady. Her name was Juna and he left Palmer and her baby.

He also fell ill and was in coma for some days. I was surprised to get a call from his parents informing me. They wanted me to visit him. I found myself going to find the husband that had left me to help him recover, which he did. After his discharge from the hospital, he returned to his new lady friend. Things did not go well for him and in the March, Juna's father had him arrested.

Nobody would bail him, so I found someone that would. My reward was that he went home and informed his parents that I conspired with two men to kill him. It was unbelievable. I wept and wept. "Ooooo, my God", if I had guessed, I would have left him to rot in jail, but for the sake of my children, I had saved their father.

The following Sunday morning, I received the SMS that changed my life gradually forever. In that SMS, he called me a non-entity, an idiot, a religious manipulator, and said woman, you are a loser, you are finished and a goner and I cease to be your husband. I will see you in court.

Could he finish me in this way? No, I am strong. He is only a mortal like me. His only privileged is to be a man, in a male dominated society. It did not stop me seeing myself as a ruined building, filled with debris and dirt, which needs cleaning and rebuilding to repair the "Walls of my Life". I feel depressed when I see sweet couples walk by. Why is that not my life?

I began my project to build a 4 bedrooms flat for my family, I completed it two years later and in July 2012 moved in with my boys. During this period, I realised I still wallowing in a pit of self-pity and it was draining my life away. He was living a life as if the world belonged to him. I told myself, "you have a life to live and no man is indispensable."

I asked myself, "are you going to move on or keep on crying?" So, began my recovery, I began to build my human relationships with colleagues. As I started relating to people and was free to interact, he became jealous and angry. I am not sure what his emotion was. Maybe it was hatred to see this person he had dominated recovering and starting to lead a normal life again. It caused him pain to see me. He could not affect me so he did the next best thing, he directed his anger at those who rendered assistance to me, including students and colleagues.

If a colleague chatted with me, that person would become his enemy.

To my joy, I worked hard from 2010 and reached the pinnacle of my career, got appointed as the administrative head of my school, a post I still hold today. It has provided me with enough income to buy a car last year.

Throughout my life, irrespective of how hard or sad it has become, my faith in God has never left me. It has been my foundation, my strength. My Christian faith in Christ Jesus and values it brings to me help me continue each day and I give thanks for what I receive.

I lean on the Holy Scriptures, such as Isa: 49:25-26, Ps 139:13-16 and Isa:54:11-15,17. I pour my heart to God, in prayer, praise and gratitude all at the same time. I kept treating the infection my husband left me with and take my medicines daily.

Today, I am a very happy woman with a select group of friends in whom I trust, consult, talk and laugh. We even quarrel occasionally, as it is all that makes life pleasant and lets you feel alive. Finally, as a believing Christian, my goals, values and principles are Biblically based. These have enabled me to maintain a high sense of discipline for myself, boys and home. Life is beautiful, no matter our experiences, the sun will always rise tomorrow. "Waaooo"

ABOUT THE AUTHOR

Gloria is a mother of three boys. Chief Lecturer, and Dean, School of General Education Kontagora Kwara State, Nigeria.

CONTACT

Boma.gloria72@gmail.com

BREAKING THE CYCLE
JayJay Williams: London

"We don't develop courage by being happy every day. We develop it by surviving difficult times and challenging adversity."

~ Barbara De Angelis

AN EVENING OUT

We journeyed into London last night, luckily getting a parking space just near the Dominion Theatre. Finding Henson's Bar, John, my husband of three years, and I had a lovely meal and glass of red wine before walking the short distance to the theatre. I was very excited. We were seeing The Bodyguard by Whitney Houston staring Beverly Knight as Whitney Houston.

We were seated in the second row from the front. The eldest of three sons, Luke, all from a previous relationship that lasted seventeen years, had booked the tickets as a present for my 50th birthday.

As I sat in the theatre watching the performance, I questioned the reality of my being and how far I had come since I was taken ill a few years ago. Nobody would believe that I was the same person today as that person, paralysed in a wheelchair. Two years ago, my body became numb from my neck down through spinal stenosis. I had no feeling or connection with the arms and hands, I felt a burning sensation coming from them. It was as if I was pinned down by heavy blocks and trapped in concrete. My brain was not making the connections to my body parts anymore. I was petrified. I did not want my boys to see me like this, I was all they had!

CHRISTMAS 2014

Bang .... Joseph pulled a Christmas cracker. I had just arrived home after being in hospital for six weeks. It was Christmas Eve and my birthday. I had undergone an emergency spinal operation and was now recovering at home for the festive period.

I loved Christmas and so did the boys. We always made it special, playing lots of music and games. We knew how to celebrate in style. It was a time to share happily together and be grateful for our love.

Within a day or two of being home, I began to feel unwell again and thought something was seriously wrong. I was dropping things again and losing feeling in my arms and legs. I did not want to worry anyone, least of all now, so I just continued with the morphine patches and pain killers. I suffered in silence hoping things would improve, but that was not to be the case. The symptoms grew worse, far worse. I was paralysed again. The MRI scan showed a huge blood clot had formed in the same area that had been operated on previously, which was compressing the nerves causing the loss of feeling.

The prognosis was not good. If left untreated the pressure would result in permanent paralysis, but the operation to remove the clot was highly risky. I did not feel I had choice.

My eldest son Luke held my hand as I signed the disclaimers. The Consultant was kind, but very matter of fact while explaining the risks. It was possible the operation would not be successful leaving me with permanent nerve damage, no voice and never able to walk again! My brain was in turmoil. What was I to do? Why was this happening to me? Everything was so surreal. I was in the darkest place I had ever been.

I had only been married three months. Poor John; what a great wife I was!

I was silent for a moment. My mind ablaze! I wanted to run away screaming, but I could not even stand up. I was completely in the hands of those around me, trapped in a body that was failing me. I wasn't even able to go to the toilet myself. My dignity was gone!

Pull yourself together "woman"!!! "You have to deal with this," Be strong for your children's sake.

Luke squeezed my hand and hugged me. I was told any improvements after surgery would happen slowly. My rehabilitation would not be instant.

The surgery was a success! They did not lie about the rehabilitation. It has taken two long hard years to learn to walk again albeit with the aid of a walking stick.

BACK TO THE THEATRE

Bang.... John jumped up in his seat as the audience cheered! I laughed!! The vibrations of the gunshots, flames, lights and music could be felt through my entire body. Beverley Knight had such an amazing, tremendous voice. I enjoyed the performance immensely, which brought tears to my eyes. Nostalgia set in: I loved the inspirational Whitney Houston. She gave me strength, I felt her power, she was my idol growing up. I felt so much sorrow and sadness when she died. When I was, younger I used to dream that if I had a little girl she would be called Whitney and she would be sent to all the best performing art schools to learn to sing and dance. She would be a top artist or model and travel the world or was I wishing that life for me?

WHEN I WAS YOUNG

I was born in St Stephens Hospital, Chelsea 1966, to an alcoholic Irish mother called Mary and a Jamaican father Michael. We lived in Wandsworth. My mother told me that Michael who I never recognized as my "father or dad" was discovered to be a paedophile. He had been "messing" with both my mum's friends and the next door neighbour's children. To protect herself, my siblings and me, my mum decided to put us into a home called Beecholme in Banstead.

Unknown to her, I was abused there even more. My memories of the home were of a very cold, sterile, regimental, unloving place where I was always hungry and felt unloved. I was always petrified when I was called to the staff office and would cry for my mum. I remember one morning in particular when my sister had told me that mum was coming to take us home. I was happy all day, and that evening in bed I asked my sister why mum had not come to pick us up. She said she only said it because she wanted to cheer me up and make me happy. I cried and called her a liar. Poor Suzanne it makes me smile now. Suzanne and my brothers were always running away only to be brought back by the police. I was not that brave and was too scared to run away with them.

I have two older brothers and two sisters, Suzanne and Jaqueline (the youngest). Jaqueline was two when she was adopted and my eldest brother was sent to another home in Leeds, Yorkshire. After being in foster homes and with foster parents in Tunbridge Wells, we were finally sent home to live with my mum and our new stepdad, Simon, in Bermondsey.

ALONG CAME PAUL!

Rolling on a few years, I left school and began working. I started work as a Personal Assistant

(P.A.) for a Japanese company in the City of London. I had supervisory powers and loved my pressurised job and the respect it brought.

Paul my fiancé, the man about to be the father of my three children was a photocopier engineer. He would drop and pick me up from work every day and even turn up in my lunch hour to surprise me. I used to earn more money than him, which was great as I didn't need to rely on him as much. Rewards come with pressure, which he didn't like and he would regularly throw insults my way for doing the work I needed to complete. It was a part of my life he could not control.

Paul could be charming, well-groomed very materialistic and enjoyed the good life. I liked that he had ambition, but money was everything to him. He was so proud whenever he bought a new BMW and would spend hours cleaning it tirelessly. When friends bought similar cars, he wanted to upstage them, so he decided to buy a Porsche telling me two days prior to purchasing it. He did not appreciate me saying it wasn't suitable for a man with three sons! I should have kept my mouth shut!

Our brilliant external relationship was very false and all about image for him. He was always the perfect gentleman to me when in public, especially in front of his friends.

We had met originally at primary school in Bermondsey when I was about eight years old. The Caribbean community in Bermondsey were very close nit in those days and both our families knew each other well.

MY PAST WAS MY SECRET

I told no-one. I was not to be discussed.

I suffered with OCD.

It ruled my life. Everything had to be in order and in the correct place. Items had to be lined forward in the cupboards, shelves and fridges. The towels and toiletries lined up correctly in the bathroom.

I would cook, clean and make sure that the three boys had what they needed for school, leaving their father to do what he wanted, which mostly involved sleeping in or his own agenda. As "Mum's Taxi", I would drop them off to their various activities, either football, scouts, dance, drama and church on Sunday then back home, complete homework, bath time, dinner, prepare the boys for school and Repeat. Church made me feel good.

I portrayed the persona of perfect housewife and mum. I had been disciplined from an early age, and being in control hid that I was very shy, nervy, unconfident and had very low self-esteem. I did not feel loved, not at least by any adult. The only unconditional LOVE I felt was for and from the boys. Psychologically I was really messed up. I could not understand life or the purpose of it.

AMBITIONS

While in London, I had been scouted by a model agency and started doing some hair and fashion modelling unbeknown to Paul. When I started doing catwalk for my friend (who has now become an international fashion designer) Paul became very jealous. He did not understand and eventually made me stop.

If Paul said I could not do something, then I would always obey or face the consequences. I was not allowed to go shopping alone or it would be another argument and things would escalate. I would avoid eye contact with other men when I was out and became anxious. Other people, both male and female, young and old said I was pretty and attractive. This would infuriate him more. He would just degrade me saying that I was a big fat ugly slag or call me a fat white bitch. He knew that I was a virgin and had only ever slept with him. How could I be a white slag? I was mixed race. My clothes hid the bruises and my fake smiles hid the sadness I carried.

MENTAL TORTURE

The constant tug of war was so confusing for me. I was adored by friends and associates, yet the man I loved, the father of my children kept reiterating how ugly I was. I needed to make myself more beautiful so he could see it.

I started taking laxatives and sticking my fingers down my throat after every meal and weighing myself daily. I did lose a lot of weight in my attempt to be more attractive for him. I got painfully thin and yet he still called me fat. I started looking in the mirror and a fat person stared back. I craved love and not just by my children. Neither my mother or father had shown me any love. The father of my three beautiful boys did not show me love or respect either, I was so lost.

I would process my behaviour and my personality over and over in my head trying to make sense of it.

Was I really that ugly? Was my personality really that bad? Why was I so obnoxious to the people I wanted to be loved by?

I started seeing a Psychiatrist in secret until she decided to reschedule my appointment and rang my landline and left a message. Paul heard the answer machine, he flipped and decided it was not necessary for me to see the Psychiatrist again. If I needed to speak to anyone I should speak to him. I wanted to understand how his mind worked so I signed up for an Open University course in Psychology. My studies did not supply me with any answers.

I COULD NOT PROTECT MY CHILDREN

During this time, alternating between periods of violence and the deterioration of my body caused by my eating habits, the mental torment I was under started to reflect in my children's development. They all began showing signs of speech impediments.

As their confidence became undermined, they developed stammers and stuttering with their speech, their attendance at school suffered with frequent stomach problems, asthma, and allergies, I was always at one clinic or hospital. It was a constant battle to help them catch up on their schoolwork.

Luke now 16 had been diagnosed when he was very young with heart complications and now had a very prominent stutter. My heart would break when other people would ask why he could not speak coherently. I had no Internet then, so could not do any thorough research and never considered for one moment what turned out to be the actual cause of symptoms linked to the children's situation.

THE AWAKENING

Bang .... that clinic door closes so heavily. I was lucky enough to get another appointment with the children's Speech Therapist and they did not need to take any time off school again. "Mrs Hay! I believe your children are suffering from their speech impediments due to severe domestic violence at home."

I paused, my blood ran cold 'what do you mean?' I demanded. There is absolutely nothing wrong with our home life. My children are loved. They are completely happy and have everything they could ever need.

It was true, they did. I showered them with everything I never had as a child. How does the Speech Therapist know? I only ever told my Psychiatrist about the children's home! I put on a good act, spoke and dress well.

I never ever thought the children could hear what was going on daily. My own personal torturing I received from their dad.   Now and again possibly, but all couples argue sometimes.

I thought I had kept it a secret. I would explain away the crashing, banging and items being broken was me being clumsy and falling or tripping over, the bruises were due to the falls and my bad back. Paul used to constantly kick me in my back when he had me on the floor while pulling at my hair. He preferred hitting me there because you could not see the bruises.

I would beg him, sobbing quietly, to stop so as not to distress the boys. I wanted to protect them and at no point or time did I think or imagine that the ongoing mental and physical abuse I was enduring was affecting my children.

I thought it was a lesser price to pay for a father's love and my children's safety and security. Boy, was I wrong. I had accepted him abusing me, I was not however willing to accept it affecting my children. They needed to be protected and I was not protecting them.

I wanted to kill Paul and started dreaming of different ways, suffocation, strangulation, even having him shot! I hated him but knew he could overpower me if he woke up while I was strangling him or suffocated him and one of us would be in prison or the other dead.

THE LEAVING

On the drive home I was contemplating, I knew enough was enough, our whole life was about to change forever. Paul always had pleasure in saying he would cut my face, take everything away from me and I would be a homeless single parent and no one else would want me if I left him.

I sorted out dinner then put the boys to bed. It was heart-breaking and very emotional, but I had finally made up my mind. He looked at me sneering. "So, you want to be a single parent, okay, you will see I will make sure you have nothing", he said, to which he walked out.

Paul had become heavily dependent on heroin and crack. He would say he was going to the shop and disappear to drug dens for days. Returning, he would get paranoid and go crazy. I would beg him to stop and to go to a detox. He wanted to live this flash champagne lifestyle. No one would believe that he was addicted to drugs, he had the money and hid his addictions well.

The weekend went by as usual, Paul did what he wanted and I carried on as normal taking the boys to their classes, but eventually Sunday arrived. Paul got home as I made Jamaican rice, peas and chicken it was now afternoon. The boys were eating at the table in the dining room, so I went up the stairs to the bedroom and brought Paul some dinner. I sat down on my favourite wicker chair in front of window.

"Why do you treat me like this?", his eyes changed as he came towards me.

Splat! He had just spat the rice, peas and chicken all over my face. It was disgusting. The food was all over me dripping down my face and onto my clothes. I was totally shocked, humiliated.

My anger was engulfing me. Enough was enough. I frantically ran to the bathroom, sobbing. It had all caught up with me. I would not take any more, I was dying slowly.

I called his father, and my mother, told them both what happened and requested them to come over as I had made my decision to finally split up. After a long threatening discussion, Paul finally gave in and decided to move out, but only after I said it was for a short trial break and promised we would get back together.

Bang .... the front door closed and Paul had gone. It was as if the dark cloud had lifted and the sun came out. I remember calling Luke and played Terence Trent Derby, our favourite song, we hugged, sang and danced. We could breathe.

No more violence. We could finally smile from within and live without the worry of fear - we had broken the cycle of abuse.

The rest is to be continued in my book to be published soon.

ABOUT THE AUTHOR

Born in 1966 England's World Cup winning year, J.J Williams was one of five brothers and sisters. She experienced the hardship of a Bermondsey, South London upbringing where the norm on pub doors was no blacks, no Irish and no dogs! Being of Jamaican and Irish descent it created an identity crisis where she could not understand the racial bigotry. She had to endure 17 years of a controlling and brutally violent fiancé, when she decided to separate from him he evicted her and their 3 children onto the streets of Croydon and disowned them. She is now a happily married woman, an author and an advocate for motivating and inspiring others going through such abuse. Her careers range from P.A to actor, author to blog writer. She is now embarking on her dream trip to Thailand and India to complete her acupuncture course and healthy lifestyle so she can heal herself and others.

CONTACT

Website: http://www.healingrelationshiptrauma.com
Facebook - Jay Jay Williams
Tumblr - Healing domestic trauma
Instagram - @HealingRelationshipTrauma
Twitter- https://twitter.com/HealingTraumaUK

CATHERINE PALMER
(from an interview with her at *Woman Unleash Your Potential Telesummit*)

HOW TO CREATE THE IDEAL RELATIONSHIP

Firstly, do you want to have an ideal relationship? Don't forget yourself, look after yourself. "Ideal" is not the same as "perfect." What you find perfect for you someone else would not. You have to find what is ideal for you. Striving for perfection is trying to achieve the impossible. An ideal partner is someone who you are in love with, who loves you in return and you each find each other continually inspiring.

How much time are you willing to give up in order to find that ideal relationship?

Catherine grew up knowing that she wanted a perfect relationship, yet married someone unsuitable. He loved the whisky bottle more than her and eventually, after 20 years of marriage, the relationship ended. She worked on herself, her personality and her attitude and spent another 5 years with someone else. That relationship was sexually fulfilling but not a lot else, so that came to an end too. After 5 years of chosen celibacy, Catherine got together with her now husband Valentine and they have been together very happily for the past 20 years. They have fun and they laugh together, which is something that she wanted in her ideal relationship. They make time to be together and they share visions; it is ideal for them.

Look at past "failed" relationships. It is an opportunity to become aware of the mistakes you made. Look at what you want from a partner in a future relationship and choose it. It is easier to look at what you don't want and then choose the opposite. For example, if you don't want a partner who smokes, choose a non-smoking partner. It is simple.

Bring into your life a vision of daily life with a partner – hear it, see it, smell it, touch it, feel it. Make conscious choices, not unconscious ones.

Make affirmations in your life to bring about changes. They have to be in the present tense – "I am" affirmations are the best. You are trying to bring something into being something new, that you have not had before. Even through failure, there can be success.

Be willing to change. Never give up. Always persevere. It will happen provided you want it enough and you take the ten steps Catherine suggests. Decide to be happy and be happy.

Read self-development books and put aside some time to do it. It needs a lot of focus and patience and sometimes takes a lot of time.

Catherine shared the story of how she and her husband got together. He found it uncomfortable without any tension in their relationship at first but because Catherine had made the effort with her own personality and there wasn't any. She told him to just be happy and to enjoy their relationship together. And they have ever since.

Catherine thinks life is more difficult for a man, especially moving from one relationship to another.

She wants to encourage people to take a chance and to be in love. Not the empty, romantic type love that is shown in movies and TV ads, but the kind between two people who see life through the same eyes, going and looking in the same way. They agree on the main things in their life, they motivate each other, encourage and educate each other. They are inspiring to each other.

True love, you do have to work at it a bit, and you have to go on working at it even when you have got it.

Catherine wants to help people who are genuinely willing to motivate themselves. She is highly qualified in stress management and the healing arts and uses these to help people. She works with people via Skype, email and telephone over a three-month period and she will support them in creating that ideal relationship in their life.

Catherine learned at an early age that using the drama of tragedy she would earn attention. She learned later in life that it doesn't always have to be that way; leave the drama to the drama queens and live life with joy and happiness instead.

TEN-STEP PLAN:

1. You must have a passion to create ideal relationship.

2. You need to look at any failed relationships.

3. Awareness.

4. Know what you want in the relationship.

5. Make conscious choices now, unlike the unconscious choices of the past.

6. Have a vision of your life with your ideal partner and practice this vision.

7. Use positive affirmation in a very simple way.

8. Persevere. Never give up.

9. Decide to be happy.

10. Read self-development books.

Write to Catherine if you need any encouragement or support, and visit her website at ideal-relationship. com for testimonials and contact details. Creative women are the type of people Catherine likes to work with because she is an artist and is very creative herself. She has written a novel *An Extraordinary Gift* (which she is giving away if you write to her to ask for one: catherine@comfidence4women.com) which is a fictional way of portraying her ten-step plan.

Listen to full interview here: http://bookprojects. uk/CatherinePalmer

CONCLUSION

When the idea of this book was shared. We had an incredible response of approval from women in the Unleashed Women Community on Facebook. It was an indication that the Love Unboxed Project was timely and needed.

Not many women are courageous enough to share their untold stories so that another may find answers. I do not know where you are as you read this book. Understand that the purpose is not to share pain, but to inspire you to look within and find answers for yourself.

I love to see a young girl go out and grab the world by the lapels. Life's a bitch. You've got to go out and kick ass. — Maya Angelou

I learned many years back that, *the day you wake up, is a new day.* May today be your day of realisation. May nothing stop you from being the very best you can be. LIVE YOUR BEST LIFE NO MATTER WHAT.

Join us to transform the world. How? If this book has been a blessing to you, if you have been inspired by the content and you know of someone who need to read these life stories share this book with them. Even better, get it as a gift. So many are dying in silence. We can change that. And you can help us.

Finally, I am very happy to share that the release of the Love Unboxed Book has inspired something wonderful. An event to connect you the reader with the co-authors. Meet them in the flesh. They are real, genuine and trust me it was not easy for some of them to put pen on paper. If you would like to meet these amazing women, go to: http://loveunboxed.com/live to register your interest.

If you have any questions, please do not hesitate to reach out. The best place to reach me is in my FB Group. I look forward to hearing from you. Remember:

Life is the first gift, love is the second, and understanding the third. - Marge Piercy

Life is a progress, and not a station. - Ralph Waldo Emerson

Make today and the rest of your years best they can be. The only thing that can stop you from living life to the full is YOU!

Thank you.

Placida Acheru

ABOUT THE PUBLISHER

Placida Acheru, founder of Unleashed Women's Network and Coaching4Excellence, is a top UK Business Transformation Coach, 3x International Bestselling Author and Mentor. She is dedicated to guiding others toward taking charge of their lives, breaking through roadblocks to systematically transform their everyday into the power to create wealth.

Placida uses her own powerful story of how she has overcome significant personal obstacles to encourage and motivate others. She is a straight-talking Business Coach, who educates clients to become laser focused on their goals. She has empowered thousands of business owners across the globe to become independent, gain visibility, credibility, growing a tribe and increasing their database by over 250% to generate sustainable income streams.

Her reputation has attracted the attention of the media who have invited Placida to feature in publications and events such as digital prints (www.people.co.uk), NHS Conferences and TV shows

(Sky 182 Ben TV, OH TV and The Sporah Show). She was also listed in the Top 100 Most Influential Black People on digital/social media drawn by eelanmedia.com. She is currently hosting *Keep Your Dream Alive Radio* featured on iTunes.

Too often the vision we hold for ourselves and our lives refuse to become reality. Visualising the life, you desire and finding the journey to achieve it can seem impossible. Placida is a renowned expert to coach you through a process of self-discovery.

Placida inspires her audience through her signature events

http://womanunleashyourpotential.com
http://visionactivationworkshop.com

CONNECT WITH PLACIDA

Website: http://placidaacheru.com
Twitter: https://twitter.com/Placida_Acheru

BOOK PROJECTS.UK

On 6th January 2015, I woke up to find myself in a hospital surrounded by machines bleeping, wires attached to my body and concerned faces starring down at me. "Hello, Placida. Welcome to 2015!" I was confused. Surely it was 2014. That was my last memory. It was explained I had been in a coma for 24 days after my body reacted badly to an energy drink I sipped. This is a true story.

Still heavy dependent on the strong painkilling drugs and then having to go through the fight to ween my body off them, it took another 20 days until I could walk out of the Royal London with the aid of a frame.

As I gradually became aware of what had happened to me. "I hit me like a thunderbolt, this could have been it" buried and gone forever. I never wrote my books. Oh, my God!   All those ideas, the scribbles, the women I want to help? Have I really served? That experienced changed my focus and my business.

As humans, we carry a lot of information in the suitcase called "Experience", this information can save a life. Many have gone and never shared their life transforming stories. When we write, we heal, we grow, we discover and we become who we are born to be. This is the reason, I created Book Projects to support women to write and explore. I bring a decade of business coaching experience into the projects. The women come to write a book, they leave with an expanded mindset and the continual support of inspirational women.

Book Projects encourages building a supportive network, sharing stories and offering resources for lifestyle and business growth.

Book Projects proudly features writers from all over the English-speaking world. Some speak and write English as their first language, while for others, it's their second, third or even fourth language. Naturally, across all versions of English, there are differences in punctuation and spelling, and even in meaning.

These differences are reflected in the work Book Projects publishes, and it accounts for any differences in punctuation, spelling and meaning found within these pages. More about our publishing and marketing service can be found at: http:// bookprojects.uk/

Life goes far beyond us. We create legacies. Masterpieces that we can be proud to hand out to future generations. – Placida Acheru

HAVE A STORY?

You could become an author in the next Love Unboxed Book.

Educate and Inspire the Next Woman.

Visit our website: http://loveunboxed.com/

Did you love the book? Got some aha! Moments?

Maybe you found yourself within its pages?

Share with us on twitter. #LoveUnboxed

Follow @Book_Projects

We would love to read your reviews